18 WELLBEING HACKS
FOR STUDENTS

of related interest

The Anxiety Survival Guide
Getting through the Challenging Stuff
Bridie Gallagher, Sue Knowles and Phoebe McEwen
Illustrated by Emmeline Pidgen
ISBN 978 1 78592 641 9
eISBN 978 1 78592 642 6

The Mental Health and Wellbeing Workout for Teens
Skills and Exercises from ACT and CBT for Healthy Thinking
Paula Nagel
Illustrated by Gary Bainbridge
ISBN 978 1 78592 394 4
eISBN 978 1 78450 753 4

You Can Change the World!
Everyday Teen Heroes Making a Difference Everywhere
Margaret Rooke
Forewords by Taylor Richardson and Katie Hodgetts
Illustrated by Kara McHale
ISBN 978 1 78592 502 3
eISBN 978 1 78450 897 5

18
Wellbeing Hacks for Students

Using Psychology's Secrets
to Survive and Thrive

Aidan Harvey-Craig

Jessica Kingsley Publishers
London and Philadelphia

First published in Great Britain in 2020 by Jessica Kingsley Publishers
An Hachette Company

1

A CIP catalogue record for this title is available from the British Library
and the Library of Congress

ISBN 978 1 78775 280 1
eISBN 978 1 78775 281 8

Printed and bound in Great Britain by Clays Ltd

Jessica Kingsley Publishers' policy is to use papers that are natural, renewable
and recyclable products and made from wood grown in sustainable forests.
The logging and manufacturing processes are expected to conform to the
environmental regulations of the country of origin.

Jessica Kingsley Publishers
73 Collier Street
London N1 9BE, UK

www.jkp.com

Dedicated to the memory of Peter Crowley

Contents

Introduction   *9*

NOTICE: Verb / nəʊ.tɪs – to see or become aware of something

Wellbeing Hack 1: Name Your Emotions   **19**
Find out about the universal and compound emotions.
Develop your emodiversity.

Wellbeing Hack 2: Eat Something You're Looking At   **33**
Forget diets and thoughtless snacking. Find out how
to bring back the joy of food.

Wellbeing Hack 3: Watch Your Thoughts   **49**
Find the links between your thoughts, behaviours and emotions.
And refuse to board the catastrophe train.

Wellbeing Hack 4: Write Yourself a Lifeline   **63**
Discover the three layers of you. Find out how to be yourself
through writing your life story.

Wellbeing Hack 5: Use Music on Purpose   **77**
Treat music like fire, not like a drug. Use it for emotion
and identity development.

Wellbeing Hack 6: Stop Dating People Like Your Parents   **87**
Look back at your first intimate relationship and decide
what you need to unlearn.

ENERGIZE: Verb / ɛnədʒʌɪz – to boost energy and enthusiasm

Wellbeing Hack 7: Paint Your Broken Edges Gold   **101**
Beware of perfectionism. Embrace your own imperfection
with the ancient art of *Kintsugi*.

Wellbeing Hack 8: Sleep for Eight Hours   **111**
Discover how to use your own superpower for emotion
regulation, creativity...and fabulous looks.

Wellbeing Hack 9: Stand on a Desk   **119**
Change your personality. Become more flextrovert.
Beware of the narcissists.

Wellbeing Hack 10: Take a Forest Bath   **131**
Find out how nature's own anti-rotting agent is the antidote
to stress.

Wellbeing Hack 11: Do (Almost) Nothing   **139**
Give your brain's default mode a chance to be creative
and to discover who you are.

Wellbeing Hack 12: Take an Exercise Snack   **147**
Discover how sitting down can make you more creative. And
how to get more BDNF mechanics to fine-tune your brain.

Wellbeing Hack 13: Breathe Tactically   **155**
Find out how combat breathing calms you down.
And coffee breathing speeds you up.

CONNECT: Verb / kəˈnekt – to bring people together

Wellbeing Hack 14: Stop Liking People   **167**
They're using conditioning to make your phone addictive.
Fight back with analogue experiences.

Wellbeing Hack 15: Join (or Leave) a Group   **177**
You have multiple social identities. Make sure you're
listening to the right ones.

Wellbeing Hack 16: Ask Someone If They're Okay – Twice   **187**
Find out why kindness really does take courage.
Be vulnerable – because you're worth it.

Wellbeing Hack 17: Thank Your Way Out of Chaos   **195**
Get past guilt, familiarity and victimhood. Use gratitude
for healing, clarity, confidence, happiness, contentment,
friendship and achievement.

Wellbeing Hack 18: Hug Someone Real   **203**
Discover how human touch is dangerously powerful.
But don't play it safe with virtual touch.

Thank you...   *215*

About the Author   *217*

Notes   *219*

Introduction

I was working in a maximum-security prison and I'd just conducted my first-ever interview with a Category A prisoner. It hadn't gone well. He'd become very agitated and aggressive halfway through the interview. Luckily, the psychologist I was taking over from was with me and together we'd managed to get the prisoner out of the office without any violence. Now we were looking at the notes of the next prisoner I was due to interview. The other psychologist asked me why I was shaking, and I joked that it was because I was hungover. Like all decent lies it had an element of truth – I was drinking a lot in the evenings to cope with the isolation of living in the middle of nowhere and spending my days working with the most dangerous men in the country. But actually I was shaking because I was scared to death.

I suspect that we both knew I was lying, but we also knew that there was an unspoken rule in the prison – *never admit to being scared*. In fact, this applied to both staff and prisoners, but for different reasons. For prisoners it was a matter of survival. For staff there was a sense that, if you were scared, you probably shouldn't be working there. The problem with this is that anyone in their right mind would've been scared at some point in that environment.

This enforced silence is certainly one of the reasons why I woke up one night experiencing my first-ever panic attack. Fear doesn't go away just because you try to ignore it. So, here's the first thing to keep in mind: If you *ever* feel like you're in trouble, with anxiety or depression or any other mental health issue, you must tell people. And it needs to be face-to-face. You could start with a trusted friend if you have one, but you must also speak to a professional such as a GP or a counsellor. Some people worry that their problem isn't that bad and that they should just get on and cope with it. But there's a really simple way of checking if you are in deep-enough trouble to see a professional: As soon as you feel like you might be, then you are.

Here's why I know that this book works

For about 25 years after that first panic attack I was lucky enough not to have any serious anxiety problems. In fact, I'd pretty much forgotten about that first episode. And I had just been given a contract to write a book – *this* book. I was genuinely excited to be given the chance of doing something that felt like it could be really useful. Everything was going well. But then, about halfway through writing the book, something happened to me. I woke up one morning and there was a noise in my head. I thought it was going to fade out, but it didn't.

Then, I started looking online at comments from other people with the same condition. I discovered that it was called *tinnitus* and that I would probably have it for the rest of my life. I found this terrifying. People were talking online about the devastation of never again being able to experience silence. I didn't think I was going to be able to cope. This time the panic attacks happened during the day, often when I was surrounded by people just getting on with their day. I had no idea when they were going to happen – it felt like my body was taking over and I had no control at all. And each time the panic kicked in, it was so raw and intense that it felt like physical pain.

The first thing I did was take my own advice and ask for help from a professional therapist. She started putting me back together, because I was pretty much broken at that point. But something else had happened – the ideas I was writing about for this book had suddenly become very real because they were keeping me afloat. I started breathing tactically to control the panic – and it worked. I started writing outside to get contact with nature and watching my thoughts to try to stop fortune telling – it helped. I was taking regular walks, using music purposefully to relax, and spending time focusing on what I was grateful for rather than what I was angry about. I stopped going online so much and spent more time with my family, including as many comforting hugs as possible. And all these things really worked to slowly get me back on track.

Perhaps most strikingly, I saw the power in the *ask someone twice* hack. Because even when I was in pieces, if someone asked me how I was, I would always say, *Fine*. But a few people could see something wasn't quite right and they would say something like, *You sure?* Then I knew I could tell them.

When you say this book *works*, what do you mean?

Let's start with what this book is *not* about. It's not about trying to be *happy* all the time. When you read the chapter called 'Name Your Emotions', you'll see that the ideal thing is to experience a wide range of emotions. That's because no emotion is always *negative* or always *positive*. Sometimes in life it's absolutely right to feel sad.

No one should be afraid of that or try to suppress it – we've already seen what happens when you try to suppress feelings.

Instead of happiness, this book is about *wellbeing*. There are quite a few elements that make up wellbeing. It's about having meaning and purpose in your life, understanding and making use of your talents, and being clear about your personal convictions. It's about being able to make things happen and to feel that you're in control of your life. It's about developing strong connections with other people. And it's about identity – knowing, and accepting, who you are.[1]

The ideas in this book are based on scientific evidence which demonstrates that they can increase your wellbeing, and they're grouped into three themes. The first theme is called '*Notice*'. This is about becoming more self-aware by taking time to reflect on your thoughts, emotions and relationships. It also gets you to reflect on how you use food and music. The theme here is that life is complex, so in order to simplify it we all spend a lot of time in a kind of *autopilot mode*. Spending some time out of autopilot, consciously noticing what's going on within and around us, can have profound wellbeing effects.

The second theme is called '*Energize*'. Some of this is very much physical, rooted in sleep, nature, exercise and breathing. But it's also psychological, gaining vitality and enthusiasm from trying new things, throwing off the constraints of perfectionism and (paradoxically) taking some time to daydream.

Finally, there is '*Connect*'. The kind of relationships we form with others is central to our wellbeing. So, this is about the ways that those relationships are formed and strengthened through kindness, gratitude and human touch.

It's true that a by-product of all this will be that your general level of happiness will increase. But keep in mind that happiness is not the primary focus – it's the by-product of wellbeing.

Can anyone improve their wellbeing?

The evidence suggests that the three things which have most affect on our general level of wellbeing are *genetics, life circumstances and intentional activity*. So, to take the first of these, it's true that some people are just born with a temperament that gives them a higher level of wellbeing than others. However, if you relied only on genetics to explain the differences in wellbeing, you'd quickly realize that you only have half the answer.[2]

When psychologists first started looking at what gives people greater wellbeing, they thought things like your social status, income, gender, age, nationality and health would be really important. They also thought that life events such as childhood trauma, being involved in a serious accident, or winning a prestigious award would be really important. So, they were surprised when it turned out that there are relatively weak links between these things and wellbeing. Gradually it emerged that the reason life circumstances don't have a much stronger effect on wellbeing is that we can get used to them.[3] It might seem that you're finally going to be happy now you've got a place at your dream university. But, in fact, you find that gradually it becomes your new normal and its effect on your wellbeing fades.

But what's really exciting about the wellbeing research is the role that intentional activity plays. This is exciting because, unlike genetics, and (to some extent) life circumstances, we're talking here about the things you choose to do to improve your wellbeing. And this is where wellbeing hacks come in. Wellbeing hacks are all about intentional activity. And the reason they're so much stronger than your life circumstances in affecting wellbeing is that it's less easy for you to adapt to them – they don't gradually become ordinary and lose their effect.

For example, let's say that it's been a few months since your life circumstances changed by starting at that dream university. You realize that the excitement is beginning to wear off. But you make the decision to use a wellbeing hack, and you spend at least one moment a day walking through the grounds (just because you can), admiring the buildings or taking in the buzz of activity, and maybe consciously thanking something or someone for getting you there. It's this wellbeing hack which will help sustain the wellbeing boost you felt when you first arrived. That's because it's episodic (not constantly there in the background) and it changes each day, so it stays fresh.

It's hard to put a figure on how much impact intentional activity has on wellbeing. As figure I.1 shows, early on researchers thought that intentional activity made up about 40% of the overall effect on our wellbeing.[4] Since then researchers have been more cautious, pointing out the complex interactions between all of the elements that make up wellbeing.[5] But the basic idea stands – you can do something about your level of wellbeing. It's in your hands.

Figure I.1: What determines wellbeing?[6]

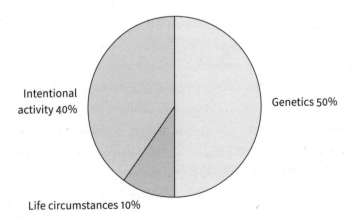

Intentional activity 40%

Genetics 50%

Life circumstances 10%

The role of *effort* – starting and maintaining

Wellbeing hacks, like any intentional activity, require some effort. And you can break this down into two parts: the *starting* and the *maintaining*. The first consideration here is to find activities that are the best possible fit with your personality.[7] That's why there's usually a range of different ways you can carry out each wellbeing hack. For example, choose between a full-on *forest bath* or taking time to enjoy a *natural view*; take a *5-minute walk* or a *20-minute high-intensity interval training* session; watch your thoughts by *refusing to board the catastrophe train* or by learning how to *doubt* them; do something different by *standing on a desk* or *taking a different route to college*, and so on.

But keep in mind what we know about adapting to life circumstances. You will get the most out of the wellbeing hacks if you vary the way you carry them out as much as possible.[8] That variety will mean that they never become ordinary and will not lose their power to make you feel great.

So, I don't wish you luck, because luck would come under life circumstances and will have little effect on your wellbeing. I wish you *intentional activity* – I wish you all the best with trying out these wellbeing hacks and finding the ideas that work for you.

NOTICE

Verb / nəʊ.tɪs

to see or become aware of something

Name Your Emotions

How do you stop yourself from acting on those heart-stopping surges of basorexia? And when was the last time you felt awumbuk? I mean really felt it deep down in your soul?

So, I'm assuming you didn't know that *basorexia* is feeling a sudden urge to kiss someone, and *awumbuk* is feeling empty after guests have left your home.[1] But just because you hadn't heard of them, does that mean you've never *felt* them? Can you feel awumbuk without even knowing it? Or maybe you have felt awumbuk but never really noticed it because you have no language to reflect on it?

How about something simpler, like sadness? If you had never heard of the word *sad*, could you still feel sad? And, if you could, how would you know that you were feeling sad? Having no word for sad might sound a bit far-fetched but we've all spent at least two years of our life without words for any of the emotions. It wasn't until you were about two years old that two parts of your brain – the *dorsolateral cortex* and the *anterior cingulate* – started to mature, and these are the drivers of verbal fluency. Only at this point did you begin to use words as symbols to represent your feelings. And this is huge. Gradually you were able to direct your attention towards how you were feeling. You could think about your emotions rather than simply experience them.[2]

But here's the thing – you couldn't make this verbal breakthrough alone. You needed a parent who was sensitive to your emotions while you were a baby and a toddler. Someone who could see when you were sad and could tell you what sadness is – maybe why it happens, how to deal with it. Someone who could tell you when they were feeling sad themselves, or read you stories about other characters feeling sad, so that you could see what sadness looks like and how it's different from other emotions like boredom or frustration. The more all this happened, the more emotion words you learned and understood.

The perfect parent (is a myth)

Perhaps, at this point, you're thinking back to your upbringing and wondering exactly how sensitive your parents were. Maybe they were often stressed. Perhaps they were often absent, either physically or emotionally. Maybe they were even abusive. But, keep in mind, your parents' ability to be emotionally sensitive to you when you were a baby is directly affected by their *own* emotion vocabulary. And, guess what, that was affected by *their* parents. This is not to excuse neglectful or abusive parenting, but if this is your experience, it can sometimes help to understand why your parents are the way they are. It can often help you to come to terms with your own feelings towards them.

Imagine your parents as toddlers, trying to work out their own emotional experiences, kind of helpless as they rely almost entirely on their parents to help them. Did they get all the support they needed? Were their parents sensitive to their emotional state? If you feel that your parents don't understand you (and maybe they don't even try), that's more or less direct evidence that the answer to these questions is *no*. But it's *no* for most of us to some extent, because all our parents are human and flawed. So, we need a plan to make up for what we didn't get in early childhood. We need a plan to help boost the number of emotions we can recognize and name.

The plan

It turns out that you can act like your own sensitive parent. This means you need to pay careful attention to your own emotions. And you need to learn some more emotion vocabulary. This will have a significant effect on your wellbeing. And if that sounds unrealistic, or unscientific, it shouldn't. There is now very good evidence that people who are really good at putting their own emotions into words are happier and healthier. For example, they're less likely to binge drink and self-harm,[3] they're less likely to rant on social media,[4] and they cope better when breaking up with a romantic partner.[5]

What's important here is that this is not about trying to be *happy*. Recognizing and naming your full range of unpleasant emotions is just as important for your wellbeing as naming pleasant ones. For example, let's say that Gary is starting a new job. You ask him how he's feeling about it and he says he is *scared*. Magnus, however, is able to respond quite differently. You ask him how he's feeling about his new job and you get something like: *I'm nervous, but also excited and, actually, a little bit nostalgic when I think back to the good times I had at my previous job, but I'm really grateful for this opportunity*. Magnus is able to split his feelings up – a bit like a prism splitting up light waves so that you can see all the different colours. Gary can only see a single *white light* of emotion – being scared. Magnus can see the whole spectrum of his emotions, and he can describe all the different colours. This ability to experience and identify a large range of different emotions is known as having *emodiversity*.[6] And people with high levels of emodiversity are less likely to be depressed, anxious and aggressive.[7]

Emodiversity is good for humans in the same kind of way that *biodiversity* is good for ecosystems.[8] Biodiversity is when an ecosystem has a wide range of different types of organism. This makes the ecosystem strong because a predator or disease cannot kill all the different types of organism at once. The disease might kill a certain type of plant, but there are many other types of plant which will be resistant. Similarly, experiencing a wide range of emotions makes it harder for a single emotion to overwhelm you. For Magnus, fear was just one element of his experience, so it could not overwhelm him because excitement, nostalgia and gratitude were also in his emotional ecosystem.

The good news is that you can build up your own emodiversity. That's a fact.[9,10] And here's how.

How are you?

When people ask, *How are you?*, you don't usually respond with an emotion word like *happy* or *disgusted*. That's because emotions are usually directed at something – *I'm happy about the grade I got in my essay* or *I'm disgusted at what that guy said*. The question *How are you?* is more likely to get a response like, *I'm fine*, or *I'm good, thanks* or maybe, *I've been better*. These responses are getting at something called *core affect*. You are always in some state of core affect – it doesn't require a trigger or a target. It's the most basic level of feeling, which is why it's a great place to start.

Core affect is measured along two dimensions: how *aroused* you are (as in how *alert* and *energized* you are); and how *pleasurable* your current state is. So, you can always plot your current core affect somewhere on these two axes, as in Figure 1.1.

Figure 1.1: The two dimensions of core affect.

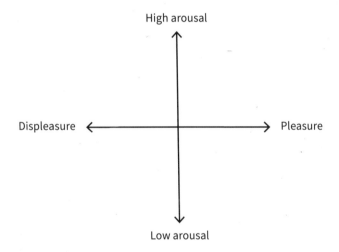

High arousal

Displeasure ← → Pleasure

Low arousal

Core affect really comes into its own when you use it as a kind of map on which you can place emotions. In fact, this map is actually called a *circumplex*.[11] But to make it all a bit more user-friendly, *The Yale Center for Emotional Intelligence* uses what they call a *Mood Meter* to map out emotions. The Mood Meter has the same two dimensions but uses the word *energy* instead of *arousal*.[12] It's divided into four sections, as shown in Figure 1.2. For example, high energy, low pleasure is the Red Zone, characterized by *anger*; high energy, high pleasure is the Yellow Zone, characterized by *happiness*.[13]

The further you travel into the corner of the Red Zone, the more *furious* the emotions become. As you travel out into the far corner of the Yellow Zone, the emotions go from simply feeling *happy* to feeling *ecstatic*. *Hopelessness* can be found at the far end of the Blue Zone, and pure *serenity* is found deep into the Green Zone. So, once you know these far reaches of the map, you can place lots of other emotions onto it.

Figure 1.2: A Mood Meter with example emotions.

There is no absolute 'right' or 'wrong' about which emotions are used or where they are placed. The point is to recognize the dimensions of 'energy' and 'pleasure' and to expand your emotion vocabulary to gain different shades of each dimension.

The RED Zone			High energy		The YELLOW Zone
Furious	Panicked	Stressed	Hyper	Excited	Ecstatic
Fuming	Angry	Frustrated	Surprised	Happy	Elated
Anxious	Annoyed	Uneasy	Relieved	Cheerful	Joyful
Despairing	Morose	Down	Satisfied	Balanced	Touched
Desolate	Sad	Bored	Restful	Calm	Peaceful
Hopeless	Depressed	Drained	Sleepy	Content	Serene
The BLUE Zone			Low energy		The GREEN Zone

Displeasure ← → Pleasure

Something about the map, and the colours, makes it all a little easier to think about and name your emotions. So, if you have lots of energy, is it *Red* energy or *Yellow* energy? Do you often find yourself in the *Blue* Zone? If so, how *Blue* are you? Acknowledging that this is the *place* in which you often find yourself can be the first step in managing what can be difficult emotions. It's also a way of getting the most enjoyment out of pleasant emotions. And, all the while that you're thinking about where you are on the Mood Meter, you are extending your emodiversity.

But, as good as the map is, you still need to know about the different emotions you can place onto it. So, then the question arises: *How many different emotion words are there?*

Universal emotions

The search for a list of universal human emotions has been going on more or less since the beginning of human civilization. For example, the ancient Chinese *Book of Rites* describes seven *qing* – that's roughly translated as *feelings* – which humans are born with. These seven feelings are *joy, anger, sadness, fear, love, disliking* and *liking*.[14]

Many centuries later, Darwin looked for universal expressions of emotion, and he came up with *anger, fear, surprise, disgust, happiness* and *sadness*.[15] This is strikingly similar to the group of emotions which Disney Pixar came up with when they produced the film *Inside Out*. There were five emotion characters inside the head of the main character Riley; the only one left out from Darwin's list was *surprise*. And that's no surprise, because there is still an argument amongst emotion researchers as to whether *surprise* really is a universal emotion, or whether it's too close to *fear* in some cultures to be distinguishable.[16]

Compound emotions

There's another group of people who are interested in identifying emotions: the tech giants such as Microsoft, Apple and Google. They are all spending huge amounts of money on artificial intelligence software to detect emotions in facial expressions. Some of the more recent research in this area has concluded that, very often, an expression does not convey a single emotion but at least two different emotions at once. These multiple emotion expressions are called *compound emotions*. Shichuan Du and Aleix Martinez, from Ohio State University, have identified 17 compound emotions, which they argue are consistent across cultures.[17]

Figure 1.3: The 17 compound emotions. The italic text indicates a bias toward that emotion.[18]

Happily surprised	Happily fearful	Happily sad	Happily disgusted
Sadly angry	Sadly fearful	Sadly surprised	Sadly disgusted
Fearfully angry	Fearfully surprised	Fearfully disgusted	
Angrily surprised	Angrily disgusted	Disgustedly surprised	
Appalled: *Disgusted* and angry	Hatred: *Angry* and disgusted	Awed: *Surprised* and fearful	

Happily fearful might be the feeling you get on a rollercoaster. *Happily sad* is the kind of bittersweet feeling you might experience when leaving home for the first time – happy to be starting a new chapter in your life but a bit sad about what you're leaving behind. Or it might be when you've been part of a school production which has just finished – after the last performance, you're happy with how it went but sad that it's all over. *Happily disgusted*, on the other hand, is the feeling you get when someone tells you a joke that's funny because it's so disgusting. That, in turn, is different from *angrily disgusted*, which you might feel at seeing some kind of injustice. Sometimes, when you build up a compound emotion, you can even give it a whole new name. For example, combining lots of *disgust* with a bit of *anger* gives you *appalled*, whereas lots of *anger* with a bit of *disgust* is called *hatred*.

To recap, what we've found is that core affect is at the foundation of your emotional experience. Then there are six basic emotions, each of which can be combined to make at least 17 compound emotions.

6, 17... Exactly how many emotions are there?

Let's take *love* as an example of why it's difficult to come up with a definitive number of emotions. Perhaps you're already wondering why something as universal as love isn't in the list of basic emotions? Paul Ekman is one of the world's leading experts on emotion research and he says that love is not an emotion because it lasts for too long. His argument is that true emotions last for minutes or even seconds, not days or weeks. *Love*, therefore, is a word to describe an emotional journey, going on for weeks, months or years. And during this journey you are likely to feel lots of real emotions, such as *excitement, jealousy, contentment* and *embarrassment*.[19]

And yet, the ancient Greeks had lots of words for *love*.[20] *Eros* was their name for the kind of love that's close to sexual desire (it's where we get the word *erotic* from). You might feel a good deal of eros when you first meet someone you're interested in. But quite quickly you'll also be looking for another kind of love in that mix – something like the love you feel for a close friend. The ancient Greeks had a name for this too – it's called *philia* and without it an intimate relationship can feel exciting but ultimately a bit unsatisfying. This is really about a *meeting of minds*, about having someone supportive and interested who is going to help you develop as a person.[21] However, it's useful also to distinguish eros from philia, otherwise a powerful flood of philia for a good friend might lead you to think that maybe you are romantically drawn to them when, in fact, you are experiencing an ancient and noble, but ultimately Platonic (quite literally), non-erotic friendship.

Then there's the unconditional, one-sided love that a parent has for a child – called *storge*.[22] You might be looking for some storge from your partner because you want them to give you some of the attention and love you missed out on as a child. Again, you might be left feeling unsatisfied if your partner is not giving this to you, even though you have never explicitly asked for it and might not even realize you need it. This need for storge in intimate relationships is why there is so often *baby talk* between partners. Even the use of the word *baby* when referring to a husband or wife clearly shows the powerful presence of storge in a relationship.

As the relationship progresses further, the chances are you're going to need some *pragma*. This is the practical (*pragmatic*) love that involves getting your combined heads down and dealing with the daily grind of working at your relationship and achieving your shared goals. This would also be the grounding on which arranged marriages have to be built, perhaps in the hope that some eros will grow out of it.

When pragma gets a bit too serious and boring, it's often useful to throw in some *ludus*. This is a playful kind of love which is all about flirting, teasing and seduction. Like all these types of love, ludus can be both positive and negative. If you're looking for some serious philia and you've met with nothing but ludus, it's time to move on. But a relationship without any ludus at all could become too intense and start to lose some of its joy.

Next there's *agape*, which is somewhere between *awe* and *empathy*. It's a kind of universal love for God or humankind which drives altruism. There's something deep-rooted about agape, which is why it has been at the heart of most religions for centuries. Catching hold of it – often by helping other people – is a source of deep contentment.

Finally, there's *philautia*, which is love of yourself. This is the driver of self-esteem and, although directed inwards, it can have a serious effect on our relationship with others. If we see no reason to love ourselves, it is very hard to see why others would love us.

This is why lists of emotions are hard to create, because it depends on whether you stop at *love* or you go all the way through these seven different types, or even come up with a few more of your own. But all of this should give you a feeling of *hope*, because what it means is that you can't really go wrong. You're not going to have a test on this because no one knows the answer. You can explore your own world of emotions and, to some extent, make it up as you go along, safe in the knowledge that the more you do, the more you'll be paying attention to your emotional life and the happier and healthier you will become.

How to develop your emodiversity

You probably already have a higher level of emodiversity, having read this chapter. That means, you're more aware of the spectrum of emotions you experience and how they map out across a circumplex. But hopefully you can also see that there are so many ways of experiencing emotion, so many different words or phrases you can use in so many different situations, that there's always an opportunity to learn more. And here are two practical suggestions to further enhance your emotional ecosystem.

The first is to read books and watch films attentively. Marcel Proust, a writer from the early 20th century, described books as a kind of *optical instrument* – something designed by the author to help the reader *see* experiences that they'd already had but failed to pay attention to, or couldn't quite put into words.[23] In other words, the whole point of stories is to help you develop your emodiversity.

This process – finding familiar emotional experiences in fictional characters – also has the further benefit of helping us realize that we are not alone in our emotional world. However dark or distressing or quirky or freakish we think our emotional ecosystem is, we can always find a character in a story somewhere who shares our experiences. And when you find this character, it can lead to *joyful relief*, or maybe *happy disgust*, but certainly less *loneliness* – because you realize that what you are feeling is shared by others.

Marcel Proust had an important condition to make about the power of stories: They unlock doors – often doors we didn't even realize were there – but it is then up to us to push the door open and go through it to discover things about ourselves. So, when a character in a story puts into words some emotional experience you relate to, there's still work for you to do in taking that insight and thinking about how and why it resonates with you. Who are the characters in your life that trigger this emotional experience? Have you had this emotional experience all your life or is it something which has been coming on gradually? Do you express it in the same way as the fictional character? Do you deal with it in the same way as the character?

The second idea to develop your emodiversity is to write an emotion diary – not necessarily every day, perhaps just when something happens that you feel the need to reflect on. Think about your experiences from life, books, films or music. Reflect on the emotions you feel and put them into words – any combination of words you like to reflect any combination of emotions you feel. The diary will give you the time and space to explore your emotional ecosystem. You can practise breaking your emotions down into beautiful landscapes of emodiversity. You'll find dark places and joyful places, calm places and manic places. Don't spend all your time in only one of these places. And don't fixate on single emotions like fear or sadness. Don't even fixate on trying only to be happy. This is about being alive. Don't miss out on any of it.

Chapter summary

★ Our childhood experiences, especially with our parents, were really important in developing a wide range of *emotion words*.

★ We can all still work on expanding the range of emotions we can name. As we do this, we are increasing our *emodiversity*.

★ Emodiversity, which includes being able to name both pleasant and unpleasant emotions, is linked to a whole host of wellbeing benefits.

★ *Core affect* is our emotional foundation. The next level is the six *universal emotions*. These can be combined to make at least 17 *compound emotions*.

★ Coming up with a definitive list of all the emotions people experience is hard. For example, is *love* a single emotion? Or should it be broken down into the seven different types of love that the ancient Greeks named?

★ Two ways to develop your emodiversity are through *attentive reading* and through writing an *emotion diary*.

Eat Something You're Looking At

When Kim Kardashian posted an Instagram picture of herself sucking on a lollipop – #suckit – Jameela Jamil responded to her post by tweeting: 'No. F**k off. No. You terrible and toxic influence on young girls.'[1]

Jameela is a former Radio One DJ who moved to LA and landed an acting role in NBC's comedy series *The Good Place*. But her story was not always so positive. At age 12 she was in a Mathematics class where the teacher weighed all the students as part of a lesson on percentages. It turned out that she was the heaviest girl in her year and this quickly became the one thing she was known for in school. That led her to stop eating properly, but it was the constant stream of media images and celebrity interviews obsessing about body image and reinforcing the *thin-is-beautiful* message which turned her anxiety into full-blown anorexia from the age of about 14.[2]

And that's why Jameela was so angry, because the lollipop that Kim Kardashian was promoting is from the *Flat Tummy Co* and it's designed to suppress your appetite, to stop you eating. So, what Jameela saw in the Kardashian Instagram post was someone making money by selling people self-consciousness about their body.

And, at the same time, selling them an idea that *not eating* is the answer. This is the same toxic message that Jameela feels pushed her into her eating disorder: *Be self-conscious, get thin, don't eat.*

So, let's get something straight: This hack is about eating, not dieting. It's about loving food, not restricting it. And it's about abandoning rules, assumptions, habits, guilt and shame.

Getting out of autopilot

Without looking at your phone, can you name the app in the top right-hand of the screen? If you're struggling to answer that, you're not alone – it's pretty easy to miss what's right in front of you.[3] When did you last think about the feel of the toothbrush on your gums, or the water on your skin as you took a shower? Have you ever thought about which shoe to put on first? And when was the last time you actually paid attention to the fact that you were walking? These experiences are likely to be so familiar that they are in some ways *automatic*.

And that's for good reason – it's necessary that we carry out a good deal of everyday life in an automatic way, because to approach everything as though it were completely new would be overwhelming. Our brains need short-cuts, so they're constantly looking for ways to hand over as much of the day-to-day information processing as they possibly can. That's why so much of our life is spent in a kind of *autopilot* mode. In fact, about 45% of everyday behaviours, including things like exercising and eating, are carried out in this automatic way.[4]

But there are problems with operating in autopilot. It can mean that we allow lots of our life to slip past unnoticed, and that's just a shame because our life is a relatively short gift and we need to make the most of it. Equally important is the fact that we can slip into behaviours and ways of thinking which are not great for our health and wellbeing. And if they're happening in autopilot mode, we don't even notice that we're doing ourselves harm.

So sometimes it's useful to force ourselves to notice what we're doing. This can help us to adapt and change. You can't make good choices if your behaviours are happening automatically. This is especially true of one of our most fundamental behaviours: eating.

Because it's so frequent and so fundamental to our everyday lives it's very easy to slip into autopilot when eating. And the problems, already highlighted, apply very much to eating. Firstly, if you're eating day in, day out without really noticing and fully experiencing what you're eating, you're missing out on some of the greatest, most delicious experiences that come with being human. Secondly, eating can easily go wrong. 34% of 16–24-year-olds in the UK are thought to be overweight or obese,[5] over a third of young adults in the USA are obese,[6] and over 1.6 million people in the UK are estimated to be affected by eating disorders.[7] So the stakes are high – this is a behaviour which is really worth paying attention to.

That's why a growing body of evidence suggests that many of us need to re-learn how to eat. Specifically, we need to learn how to eat in a *mindful* way. The essence of mindfulness is paying attention to the present moment without judgement or criticism. This is sometimes called *deautomization*[8] because it involves unravelling that automatic response – getting out of autopilot.

Here's why it's so important: Mindful eating is not about restricting food, it's not about counting calories, it's not even about losing weight. Yes, it is effective at weight management,[9,10] but more important than that, mindful eating is about maximizing the pure *joy* you can get from food.

The three eating triggers

The first thing to notice when you get out of eating autopilot is that there are three different drivers which motivate us to eat. First, there are the *physical triggers*. These are the internal cues from your body, letting you know that you're hungry, sometimes called *hunger pangs*. Second, there are *emotional triggers*. This is when you reach for a tub of ice cream because you're feeling down or bored or anxious. And finally, there are *environmental triggers*. There are a lot of different types of environmental trigger. It might be the smell of fresh bread as you walk past a bakery, or the way pastries look when they're all laid out in the window. It might be food left in the fridge or stocked up in the cupboards. It might be communal mealtimes. And it can also be things learned from childhood, such as being conditioned to eat everything on your plate, or the conditioning that came with being forced to eat some foods and forbidden from eating others.

Eat when you're hungry

Perhaps unsurprisingly, those who focus more on the physical – those who eat in response to hunger signals – are more likely to have a healthy *Body Mass Index (BMI)*,[11] which is a measure of body fat based on height and weight. So, one of the things mindful eating can do is help people to become more aware of these cues. Sometimes it takes time to re-learn how to listen to your body's hunger signals because you may have spent years ignoring them. This could be for all kinds of reasons that come under the other two types of eating trigger: emotional and environmental.

Remember, being mindful is all about paying attention in the present moment. Here, we're talking about paying attention to *your body* and listening carefully, without judgement or worry, to whether your body is telling you it needs food. There's a balance required here because this is not about waiting until you're starving, but it *is* about trying to avoid eating until you are hungry.

If you're uncertain about whether or not you're hungry, that probably means you're not hungry, so just wait a while until you know you are. Again, that sounds easy, but it may take time to master. If you feel like you're getting it wrong, keep in mind that the really important parts of this whole process are that you keep paying attention to your body and you flatly refuse to feel guilt or shame while you're trying out this new way of enjoying food.

Of course, once you decide that you are hungry, and you start eating, there's going to come a time when you're not hungry anymore. So, you need to keep the attention on your body's hunger signals as you eat and stop when you're full. In some ways, this can be even harder than deciding when to start eating. If it is an issue and you feel as though, despite your best efforts, you are constantly over-eating, you can try to estimate what you think is about the right amount to eat and put only that much on your plate. Then when it's finished, take a break by doing something completely different for 15 minutes or so (text a friend, go outside, take a shower). After the 15 minutes are up, check your body's hunger signals – are you still hungry? If so, eat some more. If not, don't.[12]

This is particularly useful for *moreish* foods. If you're human, there's likely to be at least one food that, if you start eating it, you just know you're not going to be able to stop until there's absolutely none of it left anywhere in the house. These are often foods which have been carefully designed by the food manufacturers to be as moreish as possible. That's achieved by making them tasty enough to keep you putting the food into your mouth – usually by using lots of sugar or salt – while avoiding any single, dominant flavour that would mean your body quickly figures out it's had enough.[13]

In other words, these foods are specifically designed to disrupt your body's internal hunger signals. Years of research and millions of dollars are spent finding the exact taste to make foods this addictive. You shouldn't feel guilty about falling into the traps that these researchers set.

But you can still enjoy these foods when you are hungry, without getting trapped, by using the technique above. For example, eat what you think is a reasonable amount of chocolate and then go for a walk, ideally to a specific landmark or location, so you know beforehand exactly what you're going to do. Another trick is to *start* a meal with the sweet dessert that you crave, and then go onto the savoury food – by the time you finish that, you'll have stopped the moreish craving for the sweet dessert.[14]

Eat what you truly desire – *yes, really!!*

As you become more sophisticated in reading your body's hunger signals, you need to think not just about *when* to eat but *what* to eat. This is where mindful eating has some really good news, because here's where you should abandon almost all your rules about *good* and *bad* foods. The only exception is that, if you're eating something that gets its taste from artificial flavourings, its colour from artificial dye and its texture from potassium bromate – then it's not food. So, you should not bother eating it. Think about it this way: Mindful eating puts absolutely no *real* food off-limits, so why eat chemicals?

If there are foods that you really like, do not deny yourself that food. The thing is, in order to try to avoid it, you have to pay attention to it.[15] And that can lead to increased craving. So, instead of avoiding it, take it seriously as a true luxury; if you are happy that your body is saying you are hungry for it, eat it mindfully – really paying attention to its luxuriousness.

But this is not about heading straight for your favourite foods; it's always about paying attention to your body and listening carefully to what it's telling you about what food it is hungry for. If you're struggling to hear this, try visualizing a food you think you might be hungry for.[16] Imagine the taste, the smell, the texture of it in your mouth. Do this for a minute or so and then check back with your body to see if you are still hungry for this food. Maybe try out a few different options like this – visualizing each food. Then, when you think you have it, try eating the food for real, but eat it mindfully and compare it with your visualization. Is it as satisfying as you expected? If not, is it worth trying something else? You could see this as a kind of scientific exploration to find the food that your body needs at that moment. Gradually, you'll get better at hearing your body and finding the right foods.

What's eating you?

For some people, the biggest barrier to hearing the body's hunger signals is emotion. If you find that whenever you try to eat the food you think you're craving it just never satisfies, you need to broaden your focus and pay attention to your emotions. Try to find the true source of your craving. If food is consistently failing to satisfy, then it's clear that food is not the true source of your craving.

The problem is that eating can seem as though it's helping to deal with emotions like loneliness or stress or anxiety. That means we tend to eat when we're feeling this way, even though we may not be directly aware of these underlying reasons. However, eating is always going to be a temporary fix. The emotion will soon return, and you will then need to keep eating to keep the emotion away. In fact, after a session of comfort eating like this, the negative emotion may come back even stronger because now you feel guilty too.[17]

The answer is not dieting. Dieting is likely to lead you to fixate on food and to feel the exact same negative emotions which we have just seen can cause all the problems. The answer is mindful awareness of the emotional triggers that are driving the urge to eat. This can then lead to an awareness of the difference between these emotional triggers and the internal hunger triggers of your body telling you when it is actually hungry for food. Crucially, all of this must be *unjudgemental* awareness, because, if you can avoid feeling shame about your body, you can lessen the chance of falling into the vicious cycle of emotional eating.

None of this is easy. Often, the underlying emotions which drive over-eating are difficult and painful and we do not want to acknowledge them. After all, that's the whole point of eating in the first place – to avoid dealing with them. So, try not to be overly concerned if the craving you have, which feels like hunger, is actually about something else but you have no idea what. That's fine – it's okay to not know. In fact, you should celebrate the fact that you have figured out that the craving is something other than eating. Celebrate even more if you've managed to avoid adding over-eating to whatever else is troubling you. Getting to that stage is a massive achievement.

The mindful food environment

When you buy and cook your own food, you need to bring the mindful approach with you. Be aware of any rules running through your mind as you go shopping for food. Abandon the sense of buying things because you feel you should, but also be aware of buying things that were previously off-limits just because you now can. Try to start again, from scratch, checking in with your body – what would you really like to eat today?

Most people have comfort foods that they know they're likely to go to when they feel the need for emotional eating. So, being aware of this is useful when you're buying food. Have a look at this quote in a recent study on emotional eating from McGill University in Canada, from someone interviewed about their emotional eating habits: 'Peanut butter, Nutella, those are my two big ones. So those just don't come into my apartment; and if they do, they're in little individual packages, because it's really hard to eat those without noticing.'[18]

This was not a study explicitly about mindful eating, and yet notice that this person has become aware of how they eat comfort food. They have come up with an environmental trick (using individual packages) to make sure that they notice the food they're eating, even when it's emotionally driven eating. But also keep in mind that this isn't about *limiting* the amount of Nutella that's available, it's about having plenty of it around but broken up into small packages so that you keep having to make a mindful choice to continue eating more of it or not. That's important, because limiting the availability of a desirable food in your home is actually just another form of dieting. The limitation is likely to lead to increased fixation and attention paid to that food and a greater likelihood of bingeing on it when it is available.

So, if there's a food like this which your body desires, which you find satisfying, but which you know you can get fixated on and use for bingeing in times of stress, it can be worth doing the unthinkable and actually over-stocking it in your home – having so much of it that you couldn't get through your current stock of it in one binge-session – because what you really need to do is break the idea that it's a scarce, luxurious answer to all your problems.[19]

Plates are another environmental factor that can be used to help avoid over-eating without noticing. Smaller plates lead to smaller portion sizes.[20] They may mean you go and get second helpings, but at least that's more likely to be a conscious choice. Another way to gain control is to leave a small amount of each food on your plate.[21] What this does is it helps you to think in terms of how much food you really want rather than how much the plate dictates you should have. And it's like flexing a food control muscle – you'll gradually become stronger and stronger at being able to stop eating exactly when you are full.

How to eat

Mindful eating does not come easily, but absolutely anyone can do it. You need patience to slow down and notice what you're eating. And you need to take your mind off any sense of *losing weight* or *achieving a goal*. These are not necessarily bad things in themselves but they are not part of mindful eating. You also need trust and acceptance of your own judgements about hunger and taste and emotion.

Finally, there's an element of letting go of past experiences and present attachments. This might mean letting go of feelings and behaviours associated with foods you were never allowed to eat, or were forced to eat, in the past. And letting go of negative thoughts about your body image. It also may mean letting go of eating behaviours which have become familiar coping strategies. However, letting go of the rules and restrictions will leave you free to notice how enjoyable it is to eat. And, remember, if you have the occasional mindless binge, there are no diet-police waiting to break the door down and arrest you for failing. There's just you, noticing how amazing food can be. And here's how to do it:

- *Mindful eating point 1:* Don't eat with screens or other distractions around, as you will not be able to notice the experience.[22] You need to notice every mouthful because, don't forget, you are eating exactly what your body desires.
- *Mindful eating point 2:* Before eating, try to imagine that the food in front of you is something you have never seen before. Notice what it looks like, what aromas are coming from it. Think about all the people involved in producing and cooking it.
- *Mindful eating point 3:* Take small bites and chew thoroughly. Notice the textures: *crunchy, creamy, chewy, crumbly, grainy, squidgy, fluffy, flaky, gooey, velvety.* Notice the tastes: *salty, sweet, fiery, sour, bitter, savoury, acidic, citrusy, smoky, tangy, spicy.* Again, imagine it's something like a scientific experiment – you're trying out this incredible new food to see what kind of tastes and textures you can discover.
- *Mindful eating point 4:* Make the most of those first few mouthfuls – they are the best. Even if it's your absolute favourite food, your taste buds will decrease their sensitivity after relatively small amounts.[23]
- *Mindful eating point 5:* Keep checking in with your body. Is the food still tasting amazing or have you gone into autopilot? Are you still hungry or is it time to leave some of the food on your plate? Is this food satisfying you or do you need to try something else?

Let's try that with an example food, something which you are likely to have eaten on autopilot at some time in your life – the humble *crisp* or *potato chip.* If you can, get a single potato chip in front of you right now. If not, just imagine that it's there, sitting on a plate.

Firstly, look at it. Think about the farmer who grew the potato, the sun and rain which nurtured it, the factory worker who turned the potato into a potato chip and put it into a bag of other potato chips, the lorry driver who brought it to the supermarket, the shelf-stacker who put it out on display for you to find.

Now pick it up, feel its weight. Examine its surface – the ridges and curves, the crystals of salt. Try to imagine you've never seen such a thing before. You're not trying to make yourself feel a certain way about it, you're trying to look at it as though it were a strange new object. Now smell it and notice how you react. Notice how it feels where it touches your fingers.

Now place the potato chip between your lips but just hold it there for a second or two. Pay attention to any internal messages from your body. Now put it fully into your mouth but try not to crunch down on it yet. Notice the feeling on your tongue, maybe the edges of it against the roof of your mouth.

Now, slowly, begin to crunch. Notice what each bite brings – the sounds, the changing texture and tastes. Chew the potato chip slowly like this and let it completely dissolve before you swallow. Then, after swallowing, close your eyes and notice what it feels like to have completely consumed a potato chip.

You should, by now, be looking at potato chips in a different light – appreciating each one of them as a thing of wonder. But if you're still struggling, let's go a bit deeper, further back into the history of that single potato chip...

High up in the Andes, on the shores of Lake Titicaca in Southern Peru, at the site of an ancient settlement called Jiskairumoko, archaeologists found a priceless gold and turquoise necklace thought to be nearly 4,000 years old.[24] However, something even more valuable than gold was discovered here, something which shaped the world. This is the site of the most ancient archaeological evidence of potato cultivation – it's where the ancient ancestors of your potato chip came from.[25] For thousands of years the potato remained only in this region, until 1536 when the Spanish conquered Peru. They were looking for gold, but found Peru's edible secret instead, and transported the potato thousands of nautical miles back to Spain.

The spread of the potato from Spain, across Europe, is steeped in romance and mystery, with Sir Walter Raleigh, Sir Francis Drake and Sir Thomas Cavendish all linked with its journey to England and across to Ireland, where it quickly became a staple food.[26] By the early 1700s, potatoes had found their way back across the Atlantic and were taking root in North America, transported there by Irish immigrants from Ulster.[27] Soon, potatoes had made it to the top table – Thomas Jefferson himself put potatoes on the White House dinner menu and they began to be taken seriously by all Americans.[28]

Fast forward to the 1850s and the kitchen of Montgomery Hall, a hotel in Saratoga Springs, New York. Kate Wicks was busy peeling potatoes when a potato peeling fell accidentally into a pan of fat. She fished it out with a fork and set it down on a plate. Her brother, George Crum, a chef, came into the kitchen, picked it up, tasted it and asked his sister how it had been made. She told him about the accident and he told her to keep making them.[29]

But all this is nothing compared with the story of the salt on your potato chip. While the Incas were cultivating potatoes, Chinese Emperor Hsia Yua was so desperate for salt that he went to war over access to a salt lake.[30] In ancient Greece, salt was so valuable it was used to buy slaves, leading to the expression *not worth his salt*. In Rome, soldiers were given a salt ration that became so embedded into the idea of rewarding people for their work that it led to the word *salary*.[31] Around this time Jesus Christ used salt to explain the word of God, telling his disciples that they must be the *salt of the Earth*, transforming the lives of those around them in the way that salt transforms and brings food to life. In 6th century sub-Saharan Africa, salt was as precious as gold – an ounce of gold was traded for an ounce of salt.[32] In Italy, Venice rose to economic greatness through its salt monopoly, financing the architecture, sculpture and paintings of the Renaissance. Spill salt and you might be doomed – in 1498, Leonardo da Vinci added an overturned salt cellar to his masterpiece 'The Last Supper'; it stands right in front of Judas Iscariot. And by the 1700s, in Europe, the status of your guest was determined by where they sat in relation to the silver salt cellar.[33]

So, next time you are about to eat a potato chip, think of the Inca people of Southern Peru, the Spanish conquistadors sailing home to Spain, the Irish immigrants landing in New Hampshire, Thomas Jefferson sitting down to dinner at the White House and, finally, Kate Wicks dropping a potato peeling into a pan of fat. Think about the salt crystals on it and the slaves bought for those crystals, the Roman soldiers paid in them, the gold exchanged for them. All these people and places were a necessary part of bringing you that single potato chip. That's surely worth taking a moment for – because if something with that kind of history is not worth looking at, then nothing is.

Chapter summary

★ Life is complex, so our brains go into *autopilot* when carrying out routine tasks like brushing teeth and eating.

★ Eating in autopilot is a shame because we can miss out on a lot of the joy which food can bring. It can also lead to over-eating because we're no longer listening to the *hunger signals* from our body.

★ *Mindful eating* is about getting out of autopilot and focusing your attention on what you're eating, *without judgement*.

★ Mindful eating is not about diets and food restrictions – it's about eating the foods that you *really want to eat*, but only when you're hungry.

★ If you crave food, but find that the food doesn't really satisfy you, it may be that you're eating in order to cover up an emotion you'd rather not deal with, such as *stress*, *anxiety* or *sadness*.

★ Mindful eating is about looking again at foods you've started to take for granted – as though you're seeing, smelling and tasting them *for the first time*.

Watch Your Thoughts

Do you believe that some people can look into a crystal ball and see into the future? Can you travel forwards in time and see, with your own eyes, things that have not yet happened?

Probably your answer to these questions is *no*. But then, have you ever had thoughts like these? *This is going to be a disaster. I'm not going to be able to do this assignment. He's going to let me down. I'm never going to feel better. There's nothing to look forward to, the future is hopeless.* These thoughts are all based on the idea that you have your own crystal ball, that you can see clearly into the future, and you know what's going to happen just as certainly as if you'd already seen it with your own eyes.

Take another example: Do you believe in *extrasensory perception*? That's the ability to read other people's minds. It's the idea that thoughts can be transmitted from mind to mind, even when you're in different rooms, or cities or countries. Not convinced? Then ask yourself if you've ever had any thoughts like these: *He thinks I don't know what I'm doing. She hates me now. He finds me boring.*

What's going on here? We know that no one can see into the future with complete certainty, and yet we assume we can. We know that no one can read minds, and yet we do it all the time. These are examples of *thinking errors* – types of thinking that all of us fall into at one time or another, usually without...thinking. In other words, these kinds of thought happen automatically. All we actually notice is the anxiety or depression that they create. Here's the problem: Thoughts affect emotions, and emotions affect how we behave, and our behaviour affects our thoughts. To see how this works, we're going to use an extreme example.

The blind hero

It's late evening in central London. A girl is being assaulted by two men in a doorway. Kevin Alderton is walking home when he sees that she's in trouble. Without hesitating, he rushes over, shouting to a bouncer across the street to call the police. The bouncer disappears inside but, instead of calling the police, he emerges with a gang of 20 men. These men are all friends of the attackers. Before long, Kevin is on the ground being viciously kicked and punched. Eventually Kevin escapes, badly beaten, but alive.

The next day, as Kevin is driving, he realizes there are blind spots moving across his field of vision. Then he sneezes, and his sight is gone. He pulls over to the side of the road and calls for an ambulance. Later, he finds out that both his eyes have haemorrhaged – the retinas were so badly damaged during the fight that they ripped away from the optic nerve. He is now blind. Kevin describes the aftermath of his ordeal:

> I went from a perfectly able serving soldier, enjoying life and doing the usual sort of lad stuff to suddenly being without self-confidence, having no job prospects and no self-esteem – to the point where I had no motivation to carry on my life. I was depressed and drank myself

to oblivion pretty much for three years solid because that was the only thing I saw that I could still do.[1]

We don't know his exact thoughts but we can guess some of them from the quote above: *Now I'm blind, I'm no good for anything but drinking. My life isn't worth living anymore. There's nothing to look forward to, the future is hopeless.* No one would blame Kevin for thinking this way after what he's been through. But the real problem comes when you see how these thoughts affect his emotions and his behaviour.

The thing is, if you're doing nothing but drinking to forget your problems, it becomes easier to tell yourself that you're no good for anything else. That thought, *Now I'm blind, I'm no good for anything but drinking,* becomes more and more convincing. You have evidence. Every hour in the bar is helping to prove yourself right.

In other words, Kevin's behaviour – drinking all the time – is reinforcing his negative thoughts. And his negative thoughts are making him depressed. And in order to try to escape the emotion of depression, he goes to the bar to drink. This is the vicious cycle, and it's a terrible trap to find yourself in.

Figure 3.1: All you need is doubt.

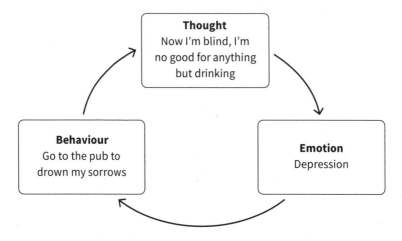

Let's return to Kevin's story. About four years after the attack, Kevin is put in touch with Billy Baxter. They have two things in common – they're both army veterans, and they're both blind. But what is special about Billy is that he set the blind solo world land-speed record on a motorbike.[2] Kevin recalls getting in contact:

> All of a sudden there was this big camaraderie thing there and then I realized that it was the camaraderie and the togetherness that I really missed from the army, and so I thought that maybe I can find it again.[3]

So, Kevin's thoughts are beginning to change: *Maybe I can find some of the camaraderie that I used to love about being in the army. Maybe my life will be worth living.* Notice that this is not an instant turnaround – he's using the word *maybe*. Kevin doesn't really know if the future will be worth living. None of us really knows what's going to happen in the future. But an important shift has happened – Kevin is no longer absolutely certain that the future is hopeless. He has doubts.

This is the best kind of doubt you can have – doubt about whether the negative voice in your head is telling you the truth. The completely black future which Kevin used to see has some cracks in it now. Those cracks are allowing a little light through, a little hope. Often, that's all that's needed.

Back to Kevin's story and he's in a bar in Italy with Billy. Yes, the drink is still there, but not exactly the same pattern of behaviour. For a start he's in Italy and, more importantly, he's in Italy to ski. This is a sport that Kevin had enjoyed since the age of eight. He'd even been a military ski instructor. But, after the accident, he was sure he'd never ski again. This is because he had that thought: *Now that I'm blind, I'm no good for anything but drinking.*

Towards the end of the night some people in the bar comment on how Kevin was skiing too fast. Right there and then he and Billy come up with an idea – Kevin will set the world's first-ever blind speed-skiing record. He gets up on the bar and announces that he'll do it next year in Les Arcs, in France.

And that's what he did. He was officially clocked at 100.54 miles per hour, although by that time he'd already fallen. The fall had slowed him down from the estimated 120 mph he'd reached before the timing zone.[4] In fact, he's the first-ever British skier to gain two world records.

Cracking the certainty of the negative thoughts was key to breaking that vicious cycle. That doubt was enough. When Kevin's thoughts turned to *Maybe*...they had less power over his emotions, so his mood lifted out of permanent depression. When the depression faded, and was replaced by hope, his behaviour started to change. He started to take chances – do things other than drink. He contacted someone who was in a similar situation and tried getting back into the sport he loved. As this behaviour changed, it became harder and harder to justify the negative thoughts. The voice in his head saying, *You're no good for anything but drinking*, was now shown to be just plain false and so it began to die away. And, as this shift in thinking happens, so Kevin's mood continues to improve – a virtuous cycle has replaced the vicious one.

Kevin's life is still going to be tough. There will be moments of depression, as there are for all of us. This is not about fairy tales and living happily ever after; it is about learning to be suspicious of the negative thoughts that sometimes appear in our heads. Learning to doubt them.

Negative automatic thoughts don't like being in the spotlight

One of the first steps to take in doubting negative thoughts is being able to notice them. They're often known as *negative automatic thoughts*. The *automatic* part is important because it means that these thoughts often seem to happen *to* us – automatically.[5] We don't even notice them. And yet we do notice the emotions and behaviours they lead to.

For example, while you're reading a textbook for an essay you have to write, you might have the automatic thought: *I don't understand this – I'm not going be able to do this essay*. That's happening while you're reading, so it's in the background, but it's still strong enough to make you feel anxious. That can lead to the behaviour of shutting the book and giving up. Now you have 'evidence' that you're not going to be able to do the essay and your negative thought is reinforced. But this may well have happened without you noticing that initial thought – the one that started it all: *I don't understand this – I'm not going be able to do this essay*.

Imagine someone else experiencing that same thought while reading the textbook: *I don't understand this – I'm not going be able to do this essay*. But this person notices that thought. They manage to get it under the spotlight. Now they can see it for what it is, and they counter it with some kind of reality check, such as *Hold on, I've been okay with most of this book, I just need to re-read this section*. Negative automatic thoughts rarely do well when you get them under the spotlight. That's why they're so good at avoiding it…

Three ways that negative automatic thoughts will try to deceive you

We've already seen that often it's the emotion which people notice rather than the thought. This means that the starting point for identifying these thoughts is to track backwards from a negative emotion to find the thought behind it. In other words, you think back to a recent time when you felt anxious or depressed and try to remember what was going through your mind. This can be even more effective if you do it in real time. That is, you catch yourself feeling anxious and then ask yourself: *What's been going through my mind leading up to this?*

You might do the same thing with behaviours. For example, you find yourself snapping at someone in anger, or staying in bed because it's safer than going out. Whatever it might be, catch yourself doing it and ask the same question: *What was going through my mind leading up to this?* With a little practice, you can start to notice these negative thoughts.[6]

However, negative automatic thoughts are not always easy to pin down. The first difficulty in dealing with them is they often seem like simple statements of fact. Sometimes they *are* statements of fact, at least on the surface. For example, *I don't understand this* may be true. But that's not what's causing the anxiety. It's the conclusion that comes with that thought which is causing the problem: *I don't understand this – therefore I'm not going to be able to do this essay.* That's where the problem is. But sometimes the first part of the thought is going to stand there convincing you it's just a fact and that you really should just get on with feeling anxious or depressed. With practice you can learn to see through it. You'll find the negative automatic thought lurking behind it – the one that's making you feel bad. That's the one you need to get under the spotlight.

Secondly, negative automatic thoughts will often present themselves in shorthand. For example, *I don't understand this – I'm not going be able to do this essay* might actually be shortened to *f**k this*, as you slam the book shut. To get the actual negative automatic thought under the spotlight, you'll need to take that shorthand and look for its underlying meaning.[7]

Finally, a negative automatic thought may not come in words at all – it might be an image. You might just see an image of the moment you're asked where the essay is. The essay you still don't have on you, and never will. You might see the frown on your teacher's face. Or the worried glances from your friends. Or people laughing about how uncomfortable you're looking. Again, these images will need to be decoded by consciously thinking about their underlying meaning.

Being able to see through these disguises and tricks is important in learning to notice your negative automatic thoughts. Noticing them is the first step – you can't doubt them unless you've noticed them.

Types of thinking error

Another way to help spot negative automatic thoughts is to learn about common types of *thinking error*. These are like thinking *traps* which we all fall into sometimes but which can become extreme and lead to us feeling distressed.[8] We've already seen two of these at the very start of the chapter. The first one is called *fortune telling* – this is when we think we know what's going to happen in the future. In fact, we're sure about it. The second one is called *mind reading* – this is when you seem to know what someone else is thinking. In fact, you're so sure, you don't even consider other, more likely, possibilities. Here are some more common thinking errors:

- *All-or-nothing thinking* is when you view a situation in only two extremes, with no middle ground. Everything is either *good* or *bad*, *success* or *failure*. Your negative automatic thoughts might include: *This essay is useless. I get rejected by everyone. Now I'm blind, I can't do anything.*
- *Must and Should statements* set your expectations unrealistically high. It's usually expectations about yourself, such as: *I must be successful. I should be getting A grades. I must keep*

my boyfriend happy. I shouldn't get stressed. But *Musts* and *Shoulds* can also involve expectations about others, such as *You must treat me well.* In fact, they can even be expectations about life in general, such as *The world must be easy.*[9] It's good to have high expectations, but what makes this kind of thinking dangerous is the way it is totally rigid. There's no room for forgiveness when you, and the people around you, fall short. That then leads to anger, resentment and depression.

- *The mental filter* involves picking out and focusing entirely on the negative elements of a situation. So, the person who gets 90% in an exam is furious about the 10% of the marks they missed: *I know she said most of my essay was great but she also said there were mistakes that had to be corrected... She must think I'm really hopeless.*

- *Disqualifying the positive* ensures that anything good can be downgraded until it's worthless: *He's only being nice to me because he wants something. That project went well because I was really lucky.*

- *Overgeneralization* is coming to a general conclusion based on a single piece of evidence. If something bad happens once, you expect it to happen again and again. This kind of thought often includes the words *always* and *never: I forgot to finish that project on time – I never do things right. This always happens to me. He didn't want to go out with me. I'll always be lonely.*

- *Taking things personally* is a thinking error that involves taking responsibility for something that's not your fault: *The relationship ended because I failed. That party didn't go well because I was nervous. She's in a terrible mood – it must have been something I did.*

- *Labelling* involves applying fixed negative traits to yourself and others. You then refuse to accept any evidence that doesn't fit with this label: *I'm ugly. He's stupid. I'm a loser.*

- *Catastrophizing* is very simple. It just means greatly over-estimating the chances of disaster: *I'm not going to be able to cope. If I can't do this essay, my life's not going to be worth living. I'm going to make a complete idiot of myself and everyone will be laughing at me. What if I forgot to lock my door and someone steals everything while I'm away? Now I'm blind, I'm no good for anything but drinking.*

All these thoughts are disturbing, but everyone has them now and then. The problem is that they can be so powerful that they seem to take us over. It's really easy to forget that they're thoughts – we can start to feel like they are *us*. They can fill us up with distress so that we seem to become the thought.

To do, or not to do, that is the question

Once you're aware of them, you'll start to notice these thinking errors. And that's the key to disarming them – to see them for what they are, to notice them as thoughts. As we've already seen, a thought is not a fact. It's a thought.

At this point there are two different routes you can take to make sure that the negative automatic thought doesn't take hold and overwhelm you. The first route is a bit like doing nothing because it involves stepping back and watching the thought pass by, like watching a train pulling away from the station.

Refuse to board the catastrophe train
Let's take catastrophizing as an example. You feel anxious and you've noticed the catastrophic thought that was behind it: *I can't*

cope. Now you need to think of this thought as a train arriving in your mind.[10] It pulls up at the station and opens its doors. Now you have a choice. Do you get on the train or not? This is the decision – do you allow that thought to carry you off? Do you go with it? Getting on the train will mean accepting that you definitely can't cope, and allowing yourself to be taken on a journey to explore every possible frightening and tragic thing which may happen in the future because of your inability to cope. You'll be able to look out of the window of the catastrophe train and see, with complete certainty, the utter bleakness of your future life – the misery and darkness and failure that is all there waiting for you.

Or...

Do you watch the catastrophe train, standing there with its doors open, and simply wait for the doors to close? Do you watch as the train pulls away without you? Taking the thought with it. Because, if you stand back and watch a negative thought, it will often move on. That's the simple magic of it. You can use any imagery that works. Sometimes people prefer to picture clouds passing by, or a stream flowing past, or birds flying, or anything that's transient – just so long as it helps you to see that you are not that thought. You are distanced from it. You can watch it pass by.

What's really important to remember is that this process is not about trying to suppress the thought or run away from it. You're not even judging the thought as good or bad at this stage. What's happening when you notice a thought, and let it pass, is quite the opposite of this. You're turning towards the thought and paying attention to it, but from a distance.

Something about not trying to suppress a thought, not trying to run away from it, seems to take a lot of its power away. It's like you're showing your own thought that you're not afraid of it. And, like an imaginary monster in a child's bedroom, when you're no longer afraid of it, it disappears.

This is not easy. Sometimes people find themselves riding the catastrophe train before they've even noticed the catastrophic thought. Kevin Alderton found this out the hard way by riding the train for three years of heavy drinking. But his story also shows that there is always hope of getting off. No matter how much a negative thought has taken hold, it's always possible to step off and begin to see it for what it is.

How to doubt your thoughts

Sometimes people feel that negative automatic thoughts just won't go away. Or, at least, they find it too hard to simply let them go. This is really where the power of doubt comes in – this is the second route to disarming negative thoughts. Again, it's important to note that this is still not about suppressing negative thoughts or running away from them or trying to pretend that everything's okay. The only goal here is to doubt the certainty of a negative thought – that's all.

Firstly, you take the negative thought and look for the evidence that does, or does not, support it. For example, perhaps you've noticed that a common thinking error you use is fortune telling. The negative automatic thoughts that come from this are things like: *There's nothing to look forward to. I'm going to be alone for the rest of my life.* Often these thoughts seem 100% rational. You are absolutely sure that the future is hopeless, because you have hard evidence – someone you love has walked out on you, or you've just had a diagnosis of a chronic illness or you've been blinded in a horrific attack.

No one's going to blame you for thinking the worst. But this is the point at which you need to look more carefully at the evidence. Because it may well be that the 'evidence' you're using is made up of things that have happened in the past. And yet you're using them to make predictions about the future. And, however certain it feels, *you do not know what the future holds.* You just don't. No one is asking you to believe that the future is going to be full of fairy tale happiness. But if the voice in your head is saying that everything is hopeless and always will be – doubt it. That voice doesn't know what the future holds any more than you do. The evidence it's using is fake.

Another useful technique for doubting negative automatic thoughts is to think of a worst-case/best-case scenario. That means taking the thought and asking: *What's the worst possible thing that could happen?* For example, you've been dumped by a boyfriend or girlfriend and the negative automatic thought is: *I can never hold onto people I love.* The worst possible consequence of this might be that you never manage to get another boyfriend; you live a long and lonely life full of solitary misery. And the best case is that you find someone absolutely perfect for you the next day and live happily ever after. Now that you've got the boundaries of the worst and best outcomes, ask yourself: *What's the most likely outcome?* It's probably not going to be the best case, but it's also probably not going to be the worst case. Somewhere between these two extremes is a more realistic guess.

This is not about having a *eureka* moment when you suddenly unmask your negative thoughts and show them to be completely fake. You're not trying to convince yourself that everything's great. You're turning the spotlight onto that voice in your head, onto that negative automatic thought. You're asking yourself: *Is it really true that being blind means I'm no good for anything but drinking? Is it really true that I never succeed? Is it really true that I can't cope with this illness? Is it really true that the future is hopeless?*

I doubt it. And so should you.

Chapter summary

★ *Thoughts*, *emotions* and *behaviours* are all linked. Negative thoughts can lead to anxiety and depression which can affect the way we behave which can reinforce our negative thoughts.

★ Often negative thoughts are *automatic* – we don't notice them. That's why they're called *negative automatic thoughts*.

★ Becoming aware of the common *thinking errors* we all slip into (such as *fortune telling* or *mind reading*) helps us to notice negative automatic thoughts.

★ One way of dealing with a negative automatic thought is simply to *observe* it and allow it to pass by.

★ Another way to deal with a negative automatic thought is to look at the *evidence* for and against it. As you do this, all that's needed is to begin to *doubt* the certainty of the thought.

Write Yourself a Lifeline

Once upon a time, there was you. In fact, there are at least three levels of you.

On the top are your personality traits – are you an *introvert* or an *extrovert*? How *narcissistic* are you? How *flextrovert* are you? You have your own combination of personality traits. A bit like a bar code, they make up a distinct pattern – the pattern of you. So, you might say things like *I'm a bit of an introvert but I do try to be open to new experiences*. And, when you say that, we all know what you mean and we can compare you with other people.

A bit deeper down are your hopes and dreams, your values, and all kinds of roles you take on. This really starts to mix things up. This is more like a painting with lots of different shapes and colours. And the image it creates (which is always changing) is an image of you. At this level, you're saying things like: *I'm a pretty hardworking student. I really want to do well so I can get a good job and make my family proud.*

But down further again – right at the heart of you – this is where your life story is being told. It's a story you tell yourself, about you. Often, you're not really aware of this story, but it's there. It's a story about your past experiences – relationships, achievements, disappointments, proudest moments, regrets... And it's a story about your fears and hopes for your future. From this story a character emerges. Sometimes it's a hero, sometimes a villain, sometimes a victim, and sometimes a winner. But mostly it's a complex mixture of all these things, and many others. That character is the person you call *you*. This is the place where you create your identity. It's an internal, evolving story of you.

Stories in liquid times

Stories are created to be told to others. They don't survive if they're not shared. That means that other people are vital in the creation of stories. Life stories are no different. Your life story is shaped by your family's story, your community's story, your country's story. For example, if your community has a history of oppression, that's going to shape your life story. Maybe your story will include something about breaking free of the oppression, or carrying the burden of your community's oppression, or of acknowledging that your story is so much better than those who have gone before you.

These other stories are important and yet, more and more, we are told to rely only on ourselves. We're told to create our own, unique life story. That's because we live in *liquid times*, where everything is uncertain and short-term.[1] It's zero-hours contracts, it's the gig economy, and it's relationships and marriages which replace *till death us do part* with *until further notice*.[2] Living in liquid times can be exciting, energizing and liberating. After all, your life story used to be dictated to you – it was built on life-long occupations. It was even built into your name: *Potter, Thatcher, Smith, Baker, Cook, Mason,* and so on. But that's all changed. Now, you're told to write your life story any way you want. The only rule is that you must be true to who you *really* are.[3] That message is everywhere. It's in the songs sung by Lady Gaga – 'Born This Way', Audioslave – 'Be Yourself', Sara Bareilles – 'Brave', Jessie J – 'Who You Are', Taylor Swift – 'Shake It Off', Kacey Musgraves – 'Follow Your Arrow', and even Frank Sinatra – 'My Way'.

But what does it mean to *be yourself*? How do you hold on to a single *real* version of yourself that's flexible enough to adapt to all the different parts of your life – the best friend, the daughter, the son, the student, the employee, the Facebook friend, the Instagram profile? The answer is that, to hang on to a coherent, continuous identity, you have to create a life story strong enough to hold together all these versions of you. That story is the way to feel a strong, consistent sense of who you are. That's why the telling of this story is the most important developmental task of young adulthood.[4] It's the groundwork for being able to be yourself.

Strong life stories have clarity and detail

Think about two key moments in your life. They could be positive moments or negative ones but they have to be specific one-off moments. For example, meeting someone who became important to you, your first class in a new school, sustaining an injury, receiving important exam results, falling out with or losing someone you were close to, winning an award, doing something you really regret, or achieving something you're really proud of. This is what college students were asked to think about in a recent study, and then they were asked to write about the event, using these instructions:

> Please describe, in detail, what happened, where you were, who was involved, what you did, and what you were thinking and feeling during the event. Also, try to convey what impact this event has had on you, and why it is an important event in your life. Try to be specific and provide as much detail as you can.[5]

The researchers found a link between the way people told these stories and their wellbeing. It didn't matter if people were talking about *good* things that had happened to them or *bad* things – it was the *clarity* and *detail* that mattered. As that increased, so did the likelihood of their having higher self-esteem, greater meaning and purpose in their lives and better relationships with the people around them.[6]

Strong life stories have underlying themes

For most people, life is quite a random thing. Stuff happens – sometimes it's good, sometimes it's bad, mostly it's a mix of both. But we need to make sense of it and bring some kind of order to it. Your life story can create that order.[7] For example, strong life stories draw together the past and the present you.[8] Take this quote from Jonathan, aged 18:

> I guess I was quite a strenuous child, also to my mother… At lunchtime I used to produce these strange sounds although I knew that my mother hated it. I continued nevertheless. I believe that this was the basis for what happened at the first day at school when I hit Klaus so hard on the nose that I almost broke it. Then came elementary school, and there I was always someone who had to attract attention by acting the clown or I don't know what…[9]

This is not simply an account of various childhood experiences – it's using those experiences to make sense of his current identity. In this case, he's using the story to help deal with a part of himself that he's struggling with – a tendency to be provocative.

So, for a life story to work, past versions of you have to evolve into the present you, in a way that makes sense.[10] That's easier said than done. You need to be able to see how past versions of you – even if they're now really embarrassing – were necessary stages in the evolution and creation of your current self.[11] And you need to be able to take multiple experiences across a lifetime and see underlying themes. These themes are the threads that draw all your experiences together into a meaningful, unified pattern of *you*-ness.[12]

For example, you might find a theme that you're always expected to be academic or artistic. Or there might be a theme that you're always trying to be no bother to anyone, to keep quiet and out of people's way. Or it might be the opposite of this, and there's a theme that you're always feeling responsible for the people around you, trying to protect them. The possibilities are pretty much endless, and there will be multiple, overlapping themes.

But here's the really good part of all of this: It's the life story which *causes* the increase in wellbeing. In other words, *individuals begin to tell new stories and then live their way into them.*[13] This is great news, because it's saying that, no matter what kind of experiences you've had, when you work on clarifying your life story it will boost your wellbeing. Ultimately, it's because a strong life story is the foundation of a well-developed sense of identity.[14]

Zooming out – write yourself a lifeline

There's a simple, yet powerful, technique that can help you to clarify your own life story and look for the themes it's built on. It's called a *lifeline* and it works like this. Firstly, you need to spend some time thinking about the significant events of your life so far. This means any key turning points in your life, any high points *and* any low points. It can be tempting to ignore the low points as they're a bit painful or embarrassing to recall, but it's essential they're included.

Keep in mind that you don't have to share this with anyone else. As a rough rule, you should be looking for a life event from at least every other year or so.

Next, you need to rate each experience on a scale of -10 to +10, where -10 is an intensely negative experience, and +10 is an intensely positive experience.

On a blank sheet of paper, turned to landscape orientation, draw a horizontal line across the centre. The far left-hand side of the line can either represent your birth or the first life event you've recalled. The far right-hand side represents the age you are right now. Mark a small dot to represent each year of your life along the line so that they're spaced out fairly evenly.

Now you're ready to start adding your life events to the lifeline. Take the earliest event and decide where it should go on the line. Then, with a ruler, draw another line directly upwards (if it's a positive event) or directly downwards (if it's negative). The length of the line should correspond to the positive or negative rating you gave that event. For example, if you gave the event a -9, you should draw the line 9cm down from the horizontal lifeline. If it was a +3, the line is drawn upwards 3cm long, and so on. At the end of each positive/negative line, write the name of the event it represents. You could also colour-code the positive and negative lines and names.

Figure 4.1: A lifeline.

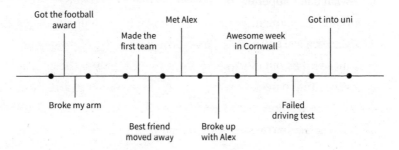

This is your starting point. And already there's plenty you can gain from your lifeline. Having all the significant events of your life represented in a graphic way like this can be helpful for seeing patterns and themes across multiple events. While you're looking at the finished lifeline, ask yourself these questions:

- Are the events bunched together in some places and spread out in others? If so, can you think of why that might be?
- Are any of the positive events only there because of negative events that went before them? What can you learn from that?
- Which people were the most involved in these big events? How are these people helping or hindering you? What can you do to maximize the influence of the people who seem to help create the positive events?
- Is there a theme underlying your positive events? Are they all academic, or social, or work-related? Are they personal accomplishments or social events?
- How about the negatives – academic or work-related? Personal or social? Some other theme?
- If you could change one thing about the lifeline, what would it be? Why would you make that change – what difference do you hope it would make to where you are now? Is there anything you can do now to make that change?
- Think again about that change – did you add something you wish had happened, or take something away that you wish hadn't happened? What can you learn from that?
- Can you see any recurring negative patterns? What can you do to break out of that and stop the pattern repeating?
- Why are the negative events negative?
    - Are they based around fear, guilt, sadness, regret, embarrassment, shame, anger?

- Can you let go of these past emotions?
- Can you be more accepting and compassionate towards your old self?
- Can your understanding of these past events help you to deal with future experiences more effectively?
- Are the events really negative, or was there something you gained or learned from them?
- Why are the positive events positive?
  - What is it that you really value in the positive events? What can you do to make more of that happen in your life?

Zooming in – writing about difficult moments

Sometimes there's a single event in the lifeline which is worth taking some time to look at on its own. For example, there's lots of evidence that writing about a difficult moment in your life is helpful. One of the first studies to show this was an experiment where people wrote about a past traumatic experience in three different conditions. The first group simply wrote down the facts – where it happened, when it happened, who was involved, etc. The second group wrote only about the emotions they felt. The third group, called the *combo* group, wrote about both the facts and the emotions. The researchers later followed up on medical records of all the people in the study and found that the *combo* group had shown a significant reduction in visits to the doctor after the writing exercise. None of the other groups showed the same reduction in visits to the doctor.[15]

Psychologists at the time were particularly excited by this finding because it used such a hard-edged objective measurement to show the effect of the writing. Since then, writing about stressful or traumatic events has been found to reduce a whole range of physical problems. Writing about migraines reduces the distress they cause.[16] Writing about the experience of living with Type I diabetes reduces the likelihood of depression.[17] Writing about arthritis-related problems results in fewer physical and emotional problems.[18] And writing about trauma in general improves immune system function.[19]

That said, there have also been studies which show the limitations of writing about trauma. For example, you need to be careful to take enough time to work through the trauma. Failing to do that risks bringing up the trauma without gaining the necessary insight to bring healing and closure.[20,21] Also, no beneficial effect has been found for people writing about their experiences of living with a negative body image,[22] with suicidal tendencies[23] or with the grief of losing a husband or wife.[24]

But, where it does work, it can have dramatic effects. And it's not just about trauma. Writing about any kind of negative event has been found to be helpful. It allows people to clarify what has happened to them, and to make sense of it. It's a bit like deciding to *own* the experience, rather than have it control you.[25,26]

Zooming forward – writing your future life story

You don't need to wait for your story to happen to you – you can write it in advance. For example, getting people to write about their *best possible self* has been shown to create all the same long-term health advantages that we've seen with writing about a past trauma.[27] The *best possible self* approach involves asking people to think about some area of their life (such as academic, social, career, or health) and imagine what it would look like if everything went as well as it possibly could. They then write about this *best possible self* for 10–15 minutes once a week over the course of at least three weeks. This simple idea has been found to increase life satisfaction,[28] mood,[29] optimism[30] and overall wellbeing.[31]

In one study, college students were given the following instructions:

> Take a moment to think about your best possible academic life during your time in college. Imagine that everything has gone as well as it possibly could. Perhaps you have successfully chosen a major or concentration that you enjoy and are achieving good grades in your classes. Think of this as the realization of the best possible academic life you could ever hope for yourself.[32]

They were then asked to write about this *best possible self* continuously for ten minutes in any kind of writing style. After that, they were asked to spend five minutes writing about specific goals that would help them make their *best possible self* story a reality:

> Now, write down a goal (or goals) you think you might want to attain that will help you achieve your best possible self that you just described. Sometimes long-term goals seem overwhelming or out of your reach. But every journey begins with just a single step. Think about taking baby steps towards your long-term goal (or goals). A baby step could be as simple as proactively seeking information you need or talking to someone who may be able to guide you. Defining the next baby step you need to take to get a little closer towards your goal is a great way to get going with the journey without worrying too much about the length of the road.[33]

Other studies have taken the same basic approach and applied it to future romantic life, hobbies or personal interests, family life, career, social life, community involvement and physical/mental health. Whatever area of life it is, people writing about their *best possible selves* show significant improvements in wellbeing, even long after the writing exercise.[34]

You're based on a true story

We're not defined by our experiences in any simple kind of way.[35] Our life story is more like a movie that's based on a true story. There are real events which shape it, but the movie is not the same as those events. So, this means that the scriptwriter has a lot of power – to make a good movie, or a bad one, an uplifting movie or a tragic one. And the scriptwriter for your life story is you. So, regardless of what has happened to you in the past, or what will happen to you in the future, you have power.

Dan McAdams has spent pretty much his whole life studying life stories. In all of that work, he has said that his most important discovery is the role of the *redemption story*.[36] Redemption stories start with something bad happening. But the story tells us how this bad thing is turned into something good. That's the redemption. Along the way to redemption, the main character may have to take a lot of hits and knock-backs, but she or he keeps going because of the hope that things will improve.[37]

There are four main types of redemption story: the *rags to riches* story, the *sin to salvation* story, the *liberation* story and the *recovery* story. The liberation story might be about literally breaking free from slavery, or it might mean breaking free from a metaphorical slavery, such as escaping from a suffocating relationship. The recovery story starts with someone losing everything. Maybe they get sick, or become addicted to drugs, or they're abused or wronged in some way. But this story ends with them fighting to get it all back.

When you start looking for redemption stories, you realize

they're everywhere, and they always have been. *Mary Magdalene's* redemption in the *Bible*, *Scrooge's* redemption in *A Christmas Carol*, *Darth Vader's* redemption in *Star Wars* and *The Grinch's* redemption from heartless despair in *The Grinch Who Stole Christmas*. There's *Maya Angelou's* liberation from racism, abuse and rape, and *Matilda's* liberation from the Wormwoods. There's *Cinderella's* fictional story of recovery from a life of subservience and abuse, and *Russell Brand's* story of recovery from a life of drugs. And so many more – some personal stories, some overarching cultural narratives.

The opposite of the redemption story is the *contamination story*. That's where something good is spoiled, ruined – contaminated – by something bad that happens after it.[38] In this story, whenever something good happens to the main character, he or she cannot enjoy it because they '*know*' that something bad will come along and spoil it.

The important thing is, people who use redemption stories for key moments in their life have higher self-esteem, greater life satisfaction and greater wellbeing. On the other hand, people who tend to use contamination stories are more at risk of depression.[39] And yet, we can all choose which of these stories to use. That's because there's almost always interpretation required to figure out if anything we experience is ultimately *all good* or *all bad*. You can contaminate good experiences and you can redeem bad ones.[40]

So, go back to the lifeline. Look at the negative events and see if you can write a redemption story around them. Let's imagine that the very last event on the lifeline is a really negative one. That could be one of two things. It could be the confirmation that no matter how good the previous events, things always turn bad. Or, that last negative event could be the start of a redemption story – it could be confirmation that things will eventually improve.

Of course, if it were easy, we would all be using redemption narratives to make our lives feel better. But it's not easy, and not everyone can do it. But sometimes, in some situations, you *can* do it, no matter how deep you've sunk. You may not have much control over what happens to you, but you *do* have control over how you choose to interpret, remember and understand it.[41] You can take a terrible event and turn it into the beginning of a redemption story. This leads to hope and progress and wellbeing. It really does.

Chapter summary

★ There are three levels of *you*. First, there are your *personality traits*. Next there are your *hopes, dreams, values* and *roles*. And then, right down at the heart of you, is your *life story*.

★ Clarifying your life story is the way to feel a strong, consistent sense of who you are – it's the key to figuring out how to *be yourself*.

★ Creating a *lifeline* is a good way to get an overview of the events in your life. From this you can find *patterns* and *themes* that clarify your life story.

★ Writing about *specific difficult events* can bring closure to them. This has been found to have a range of benefits such as reducing visits to the doctor and improving the immune system.

★ Writing about your *best possible self* leads to increased life satisfaction, mood, optimism and overall wellbeing.

★ People who use *redemption stories* for key moments in their life have higher self-esteem, greater life satisfaction and greater wellbeing. Whereas people who tend to use *contamination stories* are more at risk of depression.

Use Music on Purpose

If Pharrell Williams' song 'Happy' was constantly playing during the summer that your mother died, it could be the saddest song you know.

You might feel like you never want to hear it again. But then this might slowly change, and it might become the song that brings up bittersweet memories of your last months and weeks together. Memories that you find helpful in dealing with your grief. In time, it might become your favourite track, but not for the reasons that most people would expect – not because of its melody and beat and lyrics, but because of the memories it holds. In short, there's nothing straightforward about the way music affects us.

This should come as no surprise, because engaging with music is one of the most sophisticated things you're ever going to do. Your brain is simultaneously processing the melody, rhythm, lyrics, harmony, timbre, tempo, volume and structure of a piece of music. At the same time, it's linking these experiences to various memories and emotions that the music stirs up. It's also dealing with the way you're participating in the music – that could be listening alone, listening with others, watching a live band, composing, playing, or dancing to the music.[1]

Figure 5.1: Things your brain is processing while you experience music.[2]

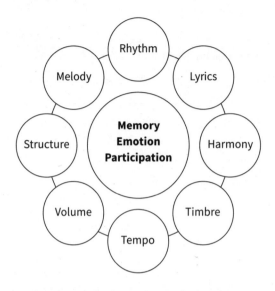

And yet, when you ask people about their experience of listening to music, it sounds simple – they will almost always talk about how music makes them feel better. People will talk about using music to relax, to get motivated, to focus, or to block out negative stuff. They talk about the way that music and lyrics help to engage with emotions and deal with difficult times.[3] But something interesting happens when you ask the *same* people to think about times when music made them feel worse. For most people, it's only at this point that they bring to mind the negative effects that music has had. What you discover is that listening to music is actually riskier than people think – it can heal, and it can hurt.[4]

Music is like fire, not drugs

The thing is, often people see music as holding all power in itself. This makes listening to music a bit like taking a drug – the music has an active ingredient which does something to you. Like this example:

> My best friend eventually just deleted the song off my phone. I was so angry at him that I didn't talk to him for two days, and if it was anyone else, I would have literally killed them. But he knows me really well, and he's been there for me through all of this crap, and so I had to forgive him. And actually, he was right. I thought that listening to that song over and over was going to make me feel better, but it didn't. It just made me feel worse and worse, but somehow, I didn't notice it. I kept hoping that if I listened enough times, and cathartically expressed my feelings, then I would pass through them and feel better in the end.[5]

This person was waiting for the music *drug* to do its magic. When it didn't seem to work, the logical conclusion was to take more of this *drug* until it did work. The problem is, it's often the people who are already distressed who are most likely to use music passively like this and allow it to make things worse.[6] These are the people who see all the power in the music, and no power in themselves. And, just like fire, when music takes control, it can be dangerous. This is not about specific genres of music or certain sub-cultures. It's about the potential for music to deepen negative thoughts and feelings.[7]

So, here's the thing: You need to use music purposefully for your own wellbeing. This active, purposeful use of music is so important it has its own name – *musicking*.[8] Musicking means listening to music with purpose and intent. The person quoted above, whose best friend deleted the song that they were stuck on, went on to say: 'I did put the song back on my phone in the end. But now I'm more conscious of what I'm doing with it.'[9] Here you can see the power-shift. Now it's the person *doing something* with the song – *using the music*. Using music in this way has all sorts of benefits, so you need to do it well. And the first step is to be clear about exactly how and why you're using music.

Using music to affect your emotions

Probably the most widely acknowledged reason for listening to music is to help us deal with our emotions.[10] The most straightforward way of doing this is for *entertainment*. Often the music is put on in the background to give us a lift or maintain a positive feeling.[11] Then, there's using music for *revival* – to relax or to energize – usually in response to feeling stressed and worn out. Thirdly, there's a strategy called *strong sensations,* which involves using music to intensify existing feelings or to generate and experience powerful feelings. This is often achieved by listening to favourite songs and is deeply affected by the voice of a singer.[12]

Almost the opposite of *strong sensations* is a strategy called *discharge* where you use music to express and release pent-up emotions. That might mean allowing yourself to cry, or release anger and frustration. The music *gives form to the expression of the current negative mood.*[13] Somehow the music expresses how you feel and just listening to it allows you to release the bottled-up emotion. Finally, there's *diversion* where the music is used to take your mind off thoughts and feelings that are troubling you. Often this might mean using music at night, to quiet your mind and help you to get off to sleep.

Figure 5.2: Five ways people use music to affect their emotions.[14]

Entertainment	Trigger pleasurable feelings
Revival	Relax and energize
Strong sensations	Intensify existing emotions
Discharge	Release pent-up emotions
Diversion	Take your mind off negative thoughts

Using music for emotional self-awareness

Music is not simply about trying to affect emotions. Often, it's more about *making sense of* complicated emotions.[15] Imagine you're breaking up with someone – you know it's the right thing to do but it's still painful because you still feel deeply for them. When you hear the same raw emotions in the lyrics and sounds of a track, it can help you to reflect on your own experiences and resolve them. This is sometimes known as *mental work.*[16]

Related to this is using music for *solace,* which is when you seek comfort and connection.[17] Often the music helps you realize that you're not alone – other people have gone through the same experiences as you, and that's comforting. It can make you feel understood.[18] Solace is also about feeling connected to important people and events, usually through memories.

Figure 5.3: Two ways that people use music for emotional self-awareness.[19]

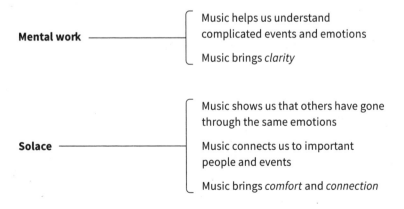

Mental work
- Music helps us understand complicated events and emotions
- Music brings *clarity*

Solace
- Music shows us that others have gone through the same emotions
- Music connects us to important people and events
- Music brings *comfort* and *connection*

Take this example, from an interview with Sarah – a girl who had lost a close friend.

Sarah: Basically it [a CD] is the one that we played as replay all summer. When we were out somewhere, we always had the player with us.

Interviewer: Has it helped you to listen to that disc?

Sarah: Yeah, it has, in a way. It brings back all the good memories to my mind basically, what we had, and all that.[20]

Using music for identity

Music can also help us to think about who we are and who we want to be.[21] Music is a mirror in which you can see ideas about yourself reflected.[22] You can see if they look good on you, or if they don't. You can play out all kinds of different versions of yourself, from the screaming maniac, to the blissful mystic and everything in-between. Listening to music is one of the few places where you can feel in complete *control* of the process of developing your own identity. Home life may be difficult, college is where you're told what to do, but your music is all yours.

At the same time as developing an individual sense of who you are, music can develop a wider, shared sense of where you fit in. This is about creating a *social identity* – it's about the family you choose, rather than the one you're given.

> You might fall down at a hardcore show and you get picked up. You can crowd surf and people catch you. It's really just a massive family, which forms out of listening to the music you love.[23]

The music provides the stories that you share with other people in your *music family*. It provides the ideas about what's important in life, and what's not important.[24] It can provide a sense of style, and ideas about what kind of clothes to wear, which then strengthens the idea of belonging, because you can see who's in your *family*.[25]

How to use music on purpose

There's a lot we can do with music, so it's worth setting aside some time and space for using it *intentionally*.[26] To do this, find somewhere comfortable where you're unlikely to be disturbed and where there are no distractions. Decide on the music you will listen to, perhaps by using a playlist so that you don't have to stop and keep finding new tracks. Think carefully about each piece of music you choose – is it there for *entertainment, revival, strong sensations, discharge* or *diversion*? Use each track intentionally for any kind of mix of these uses. Then consider whether you're trying to clarify your emotions with *mental work,* or find comfort and connection through *solace*? Can you use the track for thinking about who you are and how your identity is developing?

As the music starts, notice all the different elements of it – the melody, rhythm, lyrics and harmony. Notice the memories that the music brings back. Expand out from the music and think about the way you connect with the artist or other fans of the artist.[27] And notice the effect it's having on you. Is it having a desired effect? Or is it actually just deepening a negative mood?

Staying focused on the music will often take some practice and you may find that your mind wanders off into thoughts of its own. Try to simply notice that this has happened, without judgement – don't feel guilty or annoyed at yourself – and redirect your attention back to the music.

The girl who sang away shell shock

Music has power – it can help us all, emotionally and physically. And this isn't a new idea. Way back in 1919, news stories started appearing about *the girl who sang away shell shock*. Traumatized men were returned from war with tremors, nightmares, confusion and impaired sight and hearing. No one really knew what to do about it, but a singer called *Paula Lind Ayers* had already worked out that music could help. She'd even worked out that it was best to start with quieter, lulling songs and gradually build up to more rousing songs that the soldiers could join in with: 'I watch for signs of improvement, and when it seems wise, go on to other songs. And soon most of the boys are singing with me.'[28] In other words, music helps us to heal.

So, just like Paula, watch for signs of improvement in yourself as you use music. See your experience of using music as a series of mini experiments. Try to be flexible and adaptive, realizing that a song that brought you solace yesterday (when you were feeling relaxed) may not work the same way today (when you're feeling anxious). And be open to using different types of music, to see if they work for you, because sometimes, repeated use of just one kind of music might be the sign that you're stuck in a kind of identity loop, unable or unwilling to move forward and develop as a person.[29]

Each time you use music intentionally you'll find out more about how it works for you. You'll discover what kind of music helps in each different situation. And you'll uncover the different ways music can help your wellbeing. Like we've seen all along – there's nothing straightforward about using music. And that's the great thing about it. That's what makes music endlessly fascinating.

Chapter summary

★   Experiencing music is a complicated process. You have to simultaneously process *melody*, *rhythm*, *lyrics*, *harmony*, *timbre*, *tempo*, *volume*, *structure*, *memories* and *emotions*.

★   Using music effectively is an active thing – this is called *musicking*.

★ You can use music to *affect your emotions*, to gain greater *self-aware-ness* and for *identity formation*.

★ Listening to music on purpose requires *thinking in advance* what you want to use music for, then focusing on various different *elements* of the music experience.

★ Using music effectively requires *flexibility* and *adaptation* as you work out what kind of music experience is needed to improve your wellbeing in each new situation.

Stop Dating People Like Your Parents

Imagine you're on a blind date. Your date is lovely – really nice. But something's not quite clicking...

To explain this feeling, you have to start with two of the most infamous theories in psychology – the *Oedipus complex* and the *Electra complex*. They're controversial because they claim that very young children develop a deep-rooted, unconscious, sort-of-sexual longing for their opposite-sex parent.[1] The Oedipus complex is the boy version, suggesting that boys of around five years old have an unconscious desire for their mother. And the Electra complex is the girl version, suggesting that girls desire their father.

Even Sigmund Freud, the man that started it all off, struggled with the idea of children having anything like sexual urges for their parents. To try to explain it, he came up with the idea that real-life incest between parents and children was something which had happened in our evolutionary past, so was still present in this unconscious form as a kind of genetic hangover.[2] But this didn't help at all because neither he nor anyone else could find any evidence for incest in ancient hunter-gatherer communities, or even explain why it might have started in the first place.[3] Eventually, this all led to the Oedipus and Electra complexes being largely abandoned and discredited in contemporary psychology.

Except that some elements of these theories won't quite go away... So, why not? Why don't these theories just die?

You don't really know what you want

First of all, there does seem to be an unconscious element to attraction. Sometimes we call this *chemistry*. What this means is that the way we choose a romantic partner in real life seems to have nothing much to do with the fairy tale *ideal partner* that we construct when asked.[4] In other words, you might say you like *tall* men, but then you go for the short guy. You might say you like *kind* women, but you find the *mean* girl irresistible. Chemistry between people is not because they've found the person who ticks all their attractiveness boxes.

We can see some of this at work by flashing words on a screen and asking participants to hit the space bar as quickly as they can (within 750–1,000ms). However, they are told to hit the space bar only if they think the word on the screen is related to attractiveness (e.g. *rich, blonde, tall, slim, confident, kind*). By looking at these split-second decisions and tiny differences in reaction speed, you can assess the preferences people have before they get a chance to consciously think about them. And, what you find is that the results from this kind of test predict who you will find attractive when meeting real-life potential partners.[5]

Why you don't fancy your brother, but do act like Goldilocks

So, if you're not choosing who you find attractive on a conscious level, what is it that makes someone attractive to you? First of all, there are some evolutionary forces at work. Let's start with the good news – there is clear evidence that people brought up together as children do not feel sexual desire for each other as adults. This usually means a brother–sister relationship but it also extends to children brought up communally from birth such as those reared together in Israeli *Kibbutzim*.[6] There's a good reason for this, as mating with close family members is more likely to produce off-spring with reduced birth weight and reduced resistance to disease.[7]

However, there is also strong evidence that we choose partners who are genetically *similar* to ourselves – just as long as they're not too similar. For example, a study of over 24,000 couples found that when you know a person's genetic markers for traits such as height and body mass index (BMI) you can predict the height and BMI of their partner.[8] In other words, people have chosen partners with similar physical characteristics to themselves. In fact, the same research team found evidence that partners were similar to each other in waist-to-hip ratio, systolic blood pressure and educational attainment.

There is a logic to this – if being tall is a trait you have inherited because it is advantageous in your environment, it doesn't make much sense to find someone short to mate with. So, when we're looking for a partner, we're a bit like Goldilocks – we want someone not too similar, not too different – but *just right*.

But we've strayed quite a long way from Oedipus and Electra. In that pool of people who are just right is there any evidence that you are more attracted to people who are like your opposite-sex parent?

Well, yes, there is. But we need to break this down a bit because *like your opposite-sex parent* could mean *looks like* or *behaves like*.

Evidence that you're attracted to people who look like your opposite-sex parent

Researchers in Hungary took portrait photos of 98 wives in their early 20s. They then turned their attention to the husbands, but rather than taking a photo of the husband, they asked for a photo of the husband's mother when she was young. Then, they arranged the photos so that the picture of the husband's mother was on the left and four pictures of other women (one of which was the husband's wife) were on the right. All the photos were in black-and-white.

When they asked university students which of the four photos on the right most resembled the picture of the mother on the left, the students systematically chose the picture of the wife.[9] In other words, the men in this study were attracted to women who looked like a young version of their mother.

However, the similarity was stronger when the husband reported a close, affectionate early relationship with his mother.[10] This effect was also found the other way around, in that the emotional warmth of a father increased the likelihood that a wife's husband would resemble him.[11] And this study is not a one-off. There is also evidence that we are more likely to be attracted to people who resemble our opposite-sex parent in features such as eye colour.[12]

The Internal Working Model and partner choice

In the first few years of life, infants are very busy making sense of the new world in which they find themselves. Things like food, sleep and comfort are of primary importance and, of course, the infant is entirely dependent on their parents to supply these. So, their social world – especially interactions with parents – becomes really, really important. Over time, infant humans build up what's known as an *Internal Working Model* to make sense of this social world. This basically represents the infant's understanding of themselves (*How worthy of affection am I?*) and of the people around them (*How good are my parents at responding when I need something?*).[13]

And here's the important thing: That Internal Working Model stays with you into adult life. This is not like a computer program dictating exactly what you do in every relationship, but it's there in the background, unconsciously affecting the way you choose romantic partners. It's telling you the answers to questions such as: *How worthy of affection am I? How much can I trust other people?* It's your understanding of how relationships work.

In adulthood, it becomes more useful to think about the Internal Working Model as operating along two dimensions: *anxiety* and *avoidance*. They can help explain differences in the way we're likely to seek and respond to a romantic partner.

Anxiety

If you had parents who were really unpredictable – sometimes they would be right there for you, sometimes they would totally fail to realize you needed feeding, sometimes they would be over-protective, sometimes they would leave you on your own – that would have made you anxious. Specifically, that anxiety leads to two things. Firstly, it means that you didn't want to let your parents out of your sight because, if you did, you had no way of knowing when you might see them again. Secondly, it means that you really had to crank up the distress signals when you needed something, because your parents were not picking up on any subtle signs of discomfort or distress.

So, this is the clingy baby who cries every time they're put down or left alone, who has tantrums and hysterics. Gradually, she starts to form an understanding that important relationships are unpredictable. She learns that, to get attention from the people close to you, you have to make a fuss and grab their attention. This is their Internal Working Model – their understanding of how relationships work.

Fast forward and that same infant is now a young adult on the lookout for a romantic partner. This is the girl who is more likely to go along with unwanted sex because she learned that you have to give out completely unsubtle signals to get, and hold onto, the attention of the boys you want to get close to.[14] It's also the boy who is too intense and gets frustrated because his girlfriend won't spend every waking hour with him.[15] This is because he's learned that relationships are unpredictable and, if you let people out of your sight, you might lose them.

It's the jealous, insecure, needy person who bases their own self-worth on physical appearance and gaining compliments. It's the person whose constant need for reassurance can cause conflict with their partner. Even worse, they may also see that conflict as a *good* thing because at least it means they're getting the attention they crave.[16]

Avoidance

Let's take a different infant, with a very different early experience. This time the parents show very little affection – they are cold and distant. There is no unpredictability here, no sudden moments of affection or over-protection – just constant low-level rejection and neglect. Sometimes this comes from a parent who is, through no fault of their own, in a state of depression. This can mean that they find themselves unable to show the warmth that they would like to. But the effects are the same whatever the cause. The infant learns that it is pointless showing distress, because that never works. In fact, showing distress may even make things worse as it can make the parent angry. It's just better to avoid trying to seek affection because that's the way to minimize the chances of rejection. In short, the child learns that *self-reliance*[17] is the best way to survive.

It's not hard to see how this infant's Internal Working Model of relationships will affect them as a young adult in search of a partner. This is the girl who finds it hard to trust – and therefore commit to – a boyfriend. It's the boy who will be less caring and supportive when his girlfriend needs support, and who will be much more likely to bottle things up and not tell his girlfriend when he is suffering.[18]

This is the girl who has casual sex with someone outside of her current relationship because it has the dual benefit of being an anonymous, unemotional experience and it also reassures her that she is not dependent on her boyfriend. It's the boy who seems not to care what his girlfriend says to him but, in fact, is highly affected by small acts of rejection or criticism.[19] It's the girl who is often cynical and pessimistic about her boyfriend,[20] reacting to a surprise gift by assuming it's a sweetener which is going to be followed by some kind of admission of guilt. It's the boy who finds it hard to forgive his girlfriend, because he is less likely to believe any display of remorse.[21]

Breaking out or staying familiar

Having said all of this, it's important to remember that you are not a puppet having your emotional strings jerked around by the all-powerful Internal Working Model in your unconscious mind. You know a lot about what happened when you were young and you can make a lot of choices now about how you respond to those early experiences. We've already seen hints of this in the fact that people are only attracted to someone like their opposite-sex parent when they've had a warm relationship with that parent.

In other words, people who had a difficult relationship with parents are often looking for something completely different in a romantic partner. Sometimes this may happen unconsciously, but other times it might be a completely conscious choice to find someone who is so different that they are almost a symbolic reaction against rejected parents.[22]

But there are also some hard facts which, although they are at the extreme end of the spectrum, highlight one of the dangers of the Internal Working Model and its influence on partner choice. According to the *Office for National Statistics*, more than half of adults in the UK who were abused in some way as children enter adult relationships where they experience domestic abuse. In fact, if someone experienced multiple forms of abuse as a child – psychological, physical and sexual – this number goes up to 77%. In other words, over three-quarters of the people who experienced multiple forms of abuse as a child find an adult partner who will abuse them again.[23]

Even witnessing domestic abuse as a child in the home dramatically increases the likelihood that the same person will experience abuse by a partner as an adult (34% compared with 11% who did not witness domestic abuse).[24] These are tragic statistics, not least because you might think that someone who has experienced the trauma of abuse would be extra alert to avoiding it in the future.

But there are two main psychological explanations for this. The first is that some people have learned, as a child, that intimate relationships are abusive. That's their Internal Working Model of intimate relationships. They have learned that close relationships are abusive. This means that abusive adult relationships, although painful and horrible, nevertheless feel familiar. And that familiarity feels '*right*'.[25] Think back to the anxious person who experienced unpredictable parenting. What they learned from that experience is that they're not really worthy of love, so finding someone who will be kind and loving just doesn't fit. The person who hits them or constantly criticizes them – that's the '*correct*' fit for someone who has learned that they are pretty much worthless. That's one reason why the abused child may seek out an abusive adult partner.

The second reason is closely related but it builds on the idea of seeking out familiar patterns of '*love*'. It comes from *Imago theory*. The word Imago means *image* – the image you have of the love you received from your parents as a child. What's different about Imago theory is that it suggests that we find partners who offer us familiar '*love*' because we want to reverse the trauma of painful childhood experiences of love, to make us complete.[26]

In other words, if your father was distant and cold and you could never quite get the love you needed from him, you find a man who is distant and cold (an avoidant type) and you try to make him love you. If you can do that, everything will be okay – you will be complete and the lack of love from your father won't hurt anymore. If your father was abusive, you find an abusive partner and try to make him love you because then the trauma of your childhood abuse will be reversed and everything will be okay.

So, should I stop dating people like my parents or not?

As you can see from the evidence, the answer to this is *it depends*. If you've had a warm, loving relationship with your parents, then finding someone who resembles that warmth and love is no bad thing. If, however, you have had a difficult relationship with one or more of your parents – especially the opposite-sex parent – then you need to be more careful. You can, and should, look for a partner who will not give you the same difficulties in love. But also keep in mind that simply finding someone different from your parents doesn't necessarily make a romantic partner right for you. Rebelling for its own sake is unlikely to be productive.

The most important thing is that you are aware of your Internal Working Model of relationships. Think about what you have learned about your own self-worth and think about what you have learned to expect from close relationships. Try to forgive your parents for any shortcomings. But pay attention to the ways in which their love and care for you was not all it could have been and avoid taking refuge in the familiarity of their failings. That is, avoid seeking out a romantic partner who treats you badly just because that's what you've learned to expect. Instead, if at all possible, take the very best of any love your parents, or anyone else, have shown you and look for that. Seek out that kind of love.

Chapter summary

★ The people we find attractive in real life don't match up with the *ideal partner* we can talk about when asked, so there must be unconscious elements to attraction.

★ *Evolutionary survival* meant that it made sense to be attracted to people who are physically similar to ourselves.

★ There is evidence that the people we find attractive are likely to be similar to our *opposite-sex parent*, either physically or in the way they behave.

★ When we are very young, the relationships we have with our parents form the basis of our understanding of *how close relationships work*. This means we sometimes seek out similar relationships with romantic partners.

★ *Unpredictable parenting* can lead to *anxious adults* who need a lot of attention in a relationship, whereas *neglectful parenting* can lead to *avoidant adults* who find it hard to trust and commit.

ENERGIZE

Verb / ɛnədʒʌɪz
to boost energy and enthusiasm

Paint Your Broken Edges Gold

What do Justin Timberlake, Serena Williams and Tiger Woods have in common? Answer: They all describe themselves as perfectionists.

Right away this throws up the idea that perfectionism can be pretty good – it can get you to the top of your game, whether that's singing, dancing, tennis or golf. But for many people perfectionism is a curse.

How do I know if my perfectionism is bad?

One of the best questions to ask yourself is: *Do my high standards help me to achieve my goals or do they get in the way?*[1] For example, bad perfectionism will lead you to avoid challenges because you're scared about being exposed as an imperfect person. You're terrified of mistakes. This is a vicious cycle because it results in a person who desperately wants success but won't take the risks that are necessary to gain it.

Related to this, you can look out for perfectionist thinking. This tends to be *black-and-white* and *catastrophic* thinking.[2]

Black-and-white thinking is when you over-simplify the world into extremes – if you're not brilliant, then you tell yourself you're stupid; and if you're not fabulously beautiful, it becomes perfectly obvious that you're ugly. Catastrophic thinking is when you predict the absolute worst possible outcome: *I'm going to fail this test and then get kicked out of college and I won't be able to get a job and I'll end up on the streets.* Then, there are *Should* and *Must* thoughts, so that, even if you do achieve something good, you're ready to tell yourself: *Yeah, I got an A but I should've done more preparation for that essay. I must do better next time.*[3]

As well as thoughts, you can look out for perfectionist behaviours. Firstly, there's attention to detail. Does your perfectionism mean that you spend hours looking for typos, or arranging the font, while neglecting the overall structure and content of your essay? Do you over-prepare and excessively check? Do you constantly seek reassurance from others? Do you procrastinate and keep putting things off because you can't be sure what you're supposed to be doing will turn out perfectly? And do you fail to allow other people to help you out (because no one else will do something as perfectly as you)?

Another way to gauge if your perfectionism might be problematic is thinking about whether your sense of identity is wrapped up with your achievements.[4] That is, if you don't do as well as you would have liked, do you feel bad about what you've done or do you feel shame about who you are? For example, Joey Harrington, a former American football quarterback and self-proclaimed perfectionist, is quoted as saying: 'My value as a human being was connected to the final score. My happiness was a direct result of whether or not I lived up to the perfection of this image I'd bought into.'[5]

Keep in mind that different people can experience perfectionism in different domains of their life. The *A grade* example above is a perfectionist at college or work, but someone else might be a perfectionist in their relationships, always looking for the perfect partner. Another person might apply perfectionism to health or physical appearance, obsessively working out, checking their appearance, or filtering their selfies. And, although there might be overlap, it's possible to be a perfectionist in one domain and not in another.[6]

Why perfectionism is on the rise

In 2017 there were 229,000 cosmetic procedures carried out on patients aged 13–19 in the USA. *The American Society of Plastic Surgeons* blames much of this on the *selfie*, which, they say, exaggerates '*problems*' in features such as the nose, lip or chin.[7] Professor Simon Sherry puts it this way: 'Perfectionism is a myth and social media is its storyteller.'[8] Young people are increasingly likely to say they're being judged harshly by others and that the way to gain approval is to keep trying to perfect themselves.[9]

But why is this? Why are young people increasingly feeling the need to be perfect, to gain approval, to compare well against others? One answer lies in the modern culture of *competitive individualism*. This is rooted in the *American Dream* – the idea that success is equally available to everyone, but you must work harder than the next person in order to achieve it. In order to compete in this race for success, nothing less than striving for perfection is demanded. And the background threat is that, if you're not a high-achiever, it's your fault – you had the chance, and you blew it. Your low status becomes part of your identity, reflecting some sort of personal failure.[10]

This pressure is applied from both parents and peers. All too aware of the competition, parents can project worry and concern onto their children, leading the child to become hypersensitive and afraid of failure. Or, in their drive to ensure their children compete well, parents develop unreasonably high expectations and become overly critical, encouraging their children to strive for perfection in order to gain approval.

The dangerous faces of perfectionism

What's even more clear is that the pressure to be perfect takes its toll. The perfectionism which comes from worrying about your own unrealistically high standards is linked to anxiety,[11] anorexia nervosa,[12] depression[13] and even early death.[14] It can leave you less able to deal with stress[15] and more likely to think about suicide.[16]

Sometimes it feels like it's the people around you who are the problem. If you feel that they have unrealistically high expectations of you, it can lead to the fear that they will stop liking and respecting you when they discover your imperfections.[17] There's a vicious cycle here because this type of perfectionism mean you are less likely to seek support from those around you when you're stressed. That's understandable because seeking help is going to let everyone know that you're not perfect and you're already worried that those people will like you less when they find that out.

Sometimes the perfectionism is directed *outwards*. This is where you turn your impossibly high standards onto those around you, like your partner and your friends. People displaying this kind of perfectionism have difficulty with intimate relationships. They have much greater likelihood of conflict with their partners and lower sexual satisfaction.[18] That's because they are constantly frustrated by people failing to live up to their expectations.

Then there's *perfectionistic self-presentation*. This is an excessive drive to make sure you come across as perfect to other people.

There are actually three parts to this. Firstly, there's the need to present a flawless image to other people. Then there's also a need to avoid any situation that might highlight an imperfection. And lastly, there's the drive to *never* admit mistakes or any kind of imperfection. This type of perfectionism is especially linked to low self-esteem and social anxiety.[19] It negatively impacts on friendships and intimate relationships because it encourages dishonesty as you desperately try to sell a fake version of yourself and cover up your flaws.[20]

Perfectionism is not only dangerous, it's also boring

The word *perfect* comes from the Latin word *perfectus*, which means *to finish, to bring to an end*. So, if you really were perfect, you would be finished. Nothing more to do. You're just there, being perfect. Imagine that for a moment. You no longer have any hopes and dreams about the future; you're already perfect, so there's nothing left to hope or dream about. You don't need to ask anyone for help and advice, so there are no more conversations where you talk about life with your friends. You don't have any problems to be solved, so there's no more creative thinking. You don't have any challenges left to overcome, so there are no more moments of joy as you successfully get through a difficult time or achieve a difficult goal.

Techniques to break out of bad perfectionism

Think about what advice you'd give a friend who was in a similar position to you. The thing is, we're often much less critical of other people than we are of ourselves. So, if you find that you are giving yourself a really hard time because you got confused for a moment during a presentation – you're telling yourself what a complete failure you are for not preparing better – imagine instead that a friend of yours had done the same thing and had come to you really upset. The chances are you wouldn't have a go at your friend, telling them it was all their fault and pointing out how stupid it was to under-prepare. Instead, you'd probably tell them that it's only one moment, during one presentation, and it's not the end of the world. So, turn that reassurance back onto yourself. Because why would you treat yourself any worse than you'd treat a friend?

Then there are the perfectionist behaviours, and, although none of this is easy, this is where you can have some fun. This is where you have to practise being imperfect. Sometimes, in *Cognitive Behavioural Therapy*, these are called *behavioural experiments*. If it's helpful to think of them that way – like experiments – then use that name. So, for example, you could try opening up a little about your imperfection by telling your friends that recently you got really anxious/down/embarrassed – anything you consider to be imperfect. It's an experiment – see what their reaction is. If you're a girl who is used to looking perfect, try a day without make-up. And, on the looking-perfect theme, here's my favourite idea – leave your house wearing a piece of clothing that has a visible stain on it. Even if it's just for an hour or two. The idea you come up with should be tailored to challenge your own kind of perfectionism.[21] Your aim is to see if the world really will end because of your imperfection.

Perhaps the worst thing a perfectionist can experience is *uncertainty*.[22] Perfection requires certainty. So, working out ways to embrace uncertainty can help perfectionism. Probably the most important thing to remind yourself is that it's the people who are certain who are most often *wrong*.[23] That's pretty much certain, because it comes from a study carried out over two decades involving hundreds of experts, all trying to make predictions about uncertain events. The people who were *least* certain about their predictions were the *most* accurate. So, embracing uncertainty, in yourself as well as others, is an indication that you're realistic and more likely to be right about the future.

Taking it deeper – embracing the imperfect with *Kintsugi*

Ashikaga Yoshimasa was just 25 years old when he became *Shogun* – the military ruler of Japan. However, just four years later he decided to give up his title of Shogun altogether and concentrate on the arts. His impact on the arts is still remembered today, not because of what he created, but rather because he dropped and smashed one of his favourite bowls. Rather than throw it away, he sent this bowl to be mended. But when it was returned, it had ugly metal staples along the cracks, holding it together. He was not satisfied. This bowl meant a great deal to Yoshimasa and its repair demanded respect.

In the search to find a more elegant way to bring broken bowls back to life, the art of *Kintsugi* was developed in Japan.[24] The word Kintsugi literally means *gold-joining* and it's the practice of mending ceramics with lacquer resin and powdered gold. What this does is emphasize and celebrate the cracks on a piece of mended pottery. It's the brokenness – the cracks – which are glittering gold. And the reason for this celebration of its brokenness is that these cracks are part of the story of the piece of pottery. They are what make it unique and beautiful.[25,26] They also show that this is an object worth repairing, worth taking time over and bringing back to life, even when it may seem that it is utterly useless and broken.

We can use the process of Kintsugi to help deal with imperfection. To start with, we all face situations that make us feel imperfect and even broken. Failure, heartbreak, illness, depression, anxiety, concerns about our body – nobody can live a full life and escape all of these things. The first step in the process of Kintsugi is to pick up the broken pieces and soften any sharp edges. For us, this first means acknowledging and accepting that we're broken. Then it means taking some time to deal with any sharp, painful edges that persist. That might mean the pain of heartbreak, or the bitter disappointment of failure, or the piercing shame of something we feel is ugly about our appearance. Dealing with these things means acknowledging them – then talking to someone about them and seeking help.

The next stage of Kintsugi is to put the pieces back together. This requires patience – patience to work out how to fit the pieces back together, and patience to hold the pieces in place carefully while the resin dries. When life hits us hard, piecing ourselves back together will not be quick. But, when the resin does dry on a piece of pottery, it doesn't bring it back to its former strength, it makes it stronger.

Thus, Kintsugi involves consciously allowing the mending to be seen. When you allow your healing to be seen – like the gold paint in Kintsugi – you are not revealing weakness but rather showing that you are a person who is precious enough to be put back together. You are imperfect, and all the more beautiful because of it.

Chapter summary

★ Being a *perfectionist* can lead to high achievement. However, often perfectionism is negative because it makes people so afraid of making mistakes that they don't even try to achieve their goals.

★ *Bad perfectionism* is characterized by rigid thinking, over-preparing, procrastinating and never allowing others to help you out.

★ Perfectionism is dangerous because it is linked to *anxiety, anorexia nervosa, depression, early death, difficulty with intimate relationships, lower sexual satisfaction, low self-esteem* and *social anxiety.*

★ One way to escape perfectionist thoughts is to think about what *advice you'd give a friend* who was in a similar position to you. Then, turn that advice back onto yourself.

★ Tackling *perfectionist behaviours* is best done by practising being imperfect.

★ *Kintsugi* is a Japanese art form which highlights the beauty in imperfection.

Sleep for Eight Hours

About 90 minutes into your night's sleep, you start seeing and believing things that aren't real...

That's called dreaming and it happens mostly during *rapid eye movement (REM) sleep*. You have four to five bursts of REM sleep throughout the night, with the first one lasting only ten minutes or so and the last one lasting for over an hour. During REM sleep your eyes start flickering around under the lids, which is where it gets the name rapid eye movement, and your brain activity is almost identical to when you're awake. That means your brain is using up a lot of energy. So, there has to be something very important happening.

That something seems to be focused on dealing with difficult, emotional memories. The idea began with the work of Rosalind Cartwright, who argued that REM dreaming provides us with a safe space in which we can re-run troubling experiences. This REM dreaming gives us a chance to deal with the emotional impact of something which is troubling us, so our memories of it become less painful. It also allows us to learn from these experiences and even try out ways of resolving them.[1] As evidence, Cartwright studied recently divorced people who were struggling with depression. Those who dreamed about the stressful aspects of their divorce, and whose dreams included powerful feelings, tended to recover more effectively from the depression. She argued that this showed they were working through the divorce in their dreams.[2]

This idea has been developed by sleep researchers such as Professor Matthew Walker. Just like Rosalind Cartwright, he argues that REM dreaming is like *overnight therapy* – helping us to remember an experience but gradually lose the painful emotion it's wrapped up in. As evidence he points out that, during REM sleep, the brain's *limbic* and *paralimbic* systems are even more highly activated than when we're awake.[3] These parts of the brain are central to memory and emotion processing. At the same time, REM dreaming takes place when many of the brain's neurochemicals associated with stress (such as *noradrenaline*) are at their lowest.[4] These are the conditions during which you can re-run an emotional memory whilst stripping away the painful emotions it's wrapped up in.[5]

Sleep deprivation makes you fearful

As well as helping sort out difficult memories of past events, REM sleep helps you to cope with future life events.[6] In fact, these two things are linked. The thing is, during REM sleep, your brain goes back over troubling emotional experiences and picks out what it thinks are the most important elements.[7] If you've had an argument with someone you love, it might zoom in on an expression you noticed on their face, or the way you were feeling when things started to get heated, or a particular word or phrase they used, or the fact that it happened just after you'd had some bad news. This is really important because it makes us better at isolating that experience and clearly distinguishing it from other similar experiences in the future.[8] It means we don't spend the whole next day expecting arguments to erupt whenever we talk to people. The REM sleep has helped us work out the important, unique elements of that previous argument and we know other experiences are very different to that one.

Related to this, a lack of REM sleep makes us worse at decoding expressions in other people.[9] We can't see the subtle differences in expressions that are obvious when we're fully rested.[10] We can't tell the subtle differences between someone who is annoyed and someone who is angry. And without that ability we become increasingly fearful in response even to low-stress situations.[11] In fact, we're much more likely to worry and ruminate about stressful situations that haven't even happened yet.[12] This is why Matthew Walker describes REM sleep as a *master piano tuner*[13] fine-tuning emotional pitch. This tuning enables us to read micro-expressions appropriately and to respond appropriately to threat.

But it's not just REM sleep – recent evidence has shown that *non-rapid eye movement (NREM)*, or *slow-wave* sleep, also plays an important role in controlling anxiety.[14] The biological basis of sleep's ability to keep us emotionally balanced stems from a structure in your brain called the *amygdala* which triggers the *fight or flight* response when something stressful happens. If someone is rude to you, it's the part of your brain which is telling you to smack them in the face. However, there's another structure in your brain called the *prefrontal cortex* which deals with decision-making and impulse control. Usually, this keeps the amygdala in check, making sure you don't act too impulsively – you don't lash out. The problem is, one night of complete sleep deprivation, or just four nights of partial sleep deprivation, and your amygdala is 60% more reactive.[15] That means you're 60% more likely to lash out or run away when you're feeling threatened. And that same sleep deprivation also reduces the balancing effect of the prefrontal cortex. This means that your primitive fight or flight instincts are heightened and unchecked, making you more likely to react to the slightest provocation.

Sleep as a symptom, and as a cause

Sleep disruption is associated with pretty much every mental disorder, including clinical anxiety and depression.[16] Until recently, sleep disruption has been seen as a symptom of these disorders. But when you understand the central role sleep has in detoxing painful experiences and arming us to cope with life, it's easy to see why sleep is increasingly being seen as part of the cause of various mental disorders.[17]

Being both a symptom and a cause can quickly lead to a vicious cycle – sleep disruption leads to increased daytime symptoms, and increased daytime symptoms lead to greater night-time sleep disruption.[18] As this happens, painful memories are not properly softened by REM dreaming. And the mix of heightened emotional response and lack of impulse control keeps getting turned up. So, it's perhaps not surprising that sleep disruption also leads to an increased risk of suicidal thoughts and suicide deaths.[19]

How to sleep

With all of this at stake, it's important to know how to get a good night's sleep. And the first thing to remember is that you have to ensure a minimum eight-hour sleep opportunity each night, beginning before 11pm.[20] That probably means counting back nine hours from when you need to get up. This gives you time to drop off to sleep and allows for a little time to get up. To help this run smoothly, you should keep to a sleep schedule which is as regular as possible – getting up at the same time each morning regardless of school/college/work commitments. That includes weekends – keep them as similar to weekdays as you can.

The room you sleep in should be cool and dark, and you should avoid looking at screens for at least an hour before you intend to sleep.[21] In fact, you should try to avoid any kind of strong light during this hour run-up to sleep. What you do in bed is important. You need your brain to make a clear association between bed and sleep. So, avoid using your bed to watch YouTube videos or to text your friends – that's training your brain to see the bed as a cinema or a place to socialize. This also means that, if you wake in the night and can't sleep, you may want to get up and do something else for 20 minutes or so in a darkened room – just so you're not lying awake in bed, damaging that association of bed and sleep.

Coffee is a psychoactive stimulant that works by blocking the activity of a molecule called *adenosine*. As adenosine builds up during the day, it makes you increasingly sleepy, so blocking it with coffee basically holds back that sleepy feeling and keeps you alert. That's fine during the day, but the problem is that caffeine has a quarter life of 12 hours.[22] That means 12 hours after drinking a cup of coffee, a quarter of the caffeine will still be in your system busily doing its job and keeping you alert. Even if you do get to sleep, that sleep won't be as deep,[23] meaning you won't get the full memory and emotional health benefits discussed above.

Alcohol is also a problem for sleep. Sometimes people think they sleep better with alcohol, but alcohol is a sedative and they're mixing up sedation with sleep – the two things are not the same. Alcohol fragments sleep, causing lots of short awakenings, most of which you won't remember. Importantly, this impacts most heavily on REM sleep. No one is saying give up coffee and alcohol forever.

But, when you drink them, do it armed with the knowledge of the impact they're going to have on your sleep.

Dealing with sleep sceptics

What you will notice, if you start taking these recommendations seriously, is that there is a lot of bravado about how cool it is to function on very little sleep. If you are ever confronted with someone who is even hinting at looking down on you for needing more sleep, then please point them in the direction of the evidence above. While you're there, point out to them that less than eight hours sleep makes people uglier[24] and more likely to be obese.[25] If they are male, you could also throw in the fact that it will lead to a lower sperm count[26] and smaller testicles.[27] If they are still sceptical, point out that less than eight hours of sleep impairs the immune system[28] and is associated with higher risk of depression, anxiety, cancer, dementia, stroke, heart attack and diabetes.[29] Some people will point to high-achieving non-sleepers such as former US President Ronald Reagan and former UK Prime Minister Margaret Thatcher – they both died of dementia, which has a much higher risk if you are sleep deprived.[30]

Sometimes we get so used to the effects of sleep deprivation that we don't even realize they're there. We don't realize how much better we could feel. And yet there it is – a free super-medication which will tailor itself to our own individual experiences. Whatever is stressing you, sleep will help deal with it, and whatever ailment you might have, sleep will have a tool to fight it. Sleep is the foundation of being able to read other people's expressions, to deal with difficult situations and respond with control and dignity. Sleep is awesome. And it's free.

Chapter summary

- ★ *Rapid eye movement (REM) sleep* is like *overnight therapy.* The dreams that happen during this kind of sleep allow you to remember a difficult experience but gradually strip away the painful emotion it's wrapped up in.
- ★ REM sleep is like a *master piano tuner* – it re-tunes your ability to react to emotional experiences.
- ★ Sleep disruption is associated with clinical depression and anxiety. It used to be seen only as a *symptom*, but increasingly it's also seen as a *cause* of these disorders.
- ★ Getting the most from sleep involves ensuring you make an *eight-hour sleep opportunity*, starting before 11pm. Keeping your sleep schedule regular will also help.
- ★ Things that will disrupt sleep include *screens*, *coffee* and *alcohol*.
- ★ Getting eight hours of sleep on a regular basis is likely to make you *more attractive*, *less likely to be obese*, *more fertile*, *less likely to get sick*, *less likely to be depressed*, *less likely to be anxious*, and *less likely to develop cancer, dementia, stroke, heart disease, diabetes* and *dementia*.

Stand on a Desk

Imagine getting together with a new boyfriend or girlfriend and they pay you so much attention that you can't believe your luck. They just make you feel like you're the most special person in the world. Even when you're apart, they're always sending you texts and asking you how you are.

But then, gradually, you start to find all that attention a little bit suffocating. So, you organize a night out with your friends. And you turn the phone off. The next day, you realize your partner is not talking to you. Already you're beginning to suspect you know why. You knew in the back of your mind that they wouldn't like you meeting up with other people. Finally, it all comes out. It's not that they didn't like you going out without them, it's that they're completely *furious* that you did.

Welcome to the world of *narcissism*. You're not alone – we could be in the grip of a narcissism epidemic.[1] Narcissism is a personality trait characterized by *entitled self-importance*.[2] What this means is that people high in narcissism believe that their own needs are more important than anyone else's. You would think that no one would go near such a person but you'd be wrong.

Firstly, narcissists are perfectly happy to exploit others. That's because they see other people as nothing more than a means to getting the things they want. And what they usually want is your undivided attention, your unwavering loyalty, and your complete devotion. When someone wants these things from you, it can be quite seductive.[3] To start with...

Secondly, narcissists are vulnerable because they cannot accept looking bad in any situation. That means they are extremely preoccupied with their social image, whether online or in person.[4] They're always carefully presenting an idealized picture of who they are. And that's the version of them that you meet on first contact.

Grandiose and vulnerable narcissism

There are actually two quite different types of narcissist. *Grandiose narcissism* is expressed outwardly. Grandiose narcissists are people who have to dominate social situations. Their focus is on success and recognition, without any concern for others.[5] A common trait of the grandiose narcissist is to treat waiters badly, as though the waiter is barely human.[6]

The opposite of this is *vulnerable narcissism*, which is expressed inwardly and can therefore be a little trickier to spot.[7] People high in vulnerable narcissism are much more introverted and shy; they lack self-confidence in social settings, so it may look as though they're not self-centred at all. But they are.[8] They will tend to prefer online communication and online relationships because they have more control over what happens and can ensure their self-esteem is not threatened.[9] Also, they'll cross boundaries – like the boyfriend who constantly texts his girlfriend when she's with other people to check that he is still the centre of her attention even when they are apart.[10] And they will tend to be hostile towards your family and also towards friends you made independently of them, because, again, these people threaten their control and threaten their status as the centre of attention.[11]

Most importantly, you'll know a vulnerable narcissist when you find someone who is hypersensitive to criticism. If you're dating someone like this, you may find yourself *walking on eggshells* – that is, being really careful about what you say to them because you've gradually picked up that even the slightest criticism or difference of opinion leads to a big fall-out. Often, that fall-out will mean that they become passively aggressive, like someone who stops talking to you when they think you've paid too much attention to someone else.

Just like all forms of narcissism, the manipulative element will be there. Guilt trips such as *look at all the things I've done for you, you're so ungrateful* can be used to make unreasonable demands.[12] And these people tend to get away with this kind of behaviour because, as we've already seen, they know when to turn on the charm. When they sense that it is needed, they can make you feel very special and wanted so that you put aside your concerns because you feel indebted to them.

Uncovering personality traits

Would you describe yourself as *talkative, witty, jolly, merry, lively, peppy, articulate, verbose, gossipy, companionable, social, outgoing, impulsive, carefree, playful, zany, mischievous, rowdy, loud, prankish, brave, venturous, fearless, reckless, active, assertive, dominant, energetic, boastful, conceited, egotistical, affected, vain, chic, dapper, jaunty, nosey, snoopy, indiscreet, meddlesome, sexy, passionate, sensual, flirtatious, reserved, lethargic, apathetic, cool, aloof, distant, unsocial, withdrawn, quiet, secretive, untalkative, indirect, humble, modest, bashful, meek, shy, joyless, solemn, sober, morose, moody, tactless, thoughtless, unfriendly, trustful, unsuspicious, unenvious, democratic, friendly, genial, cheerful, generous, charitable, indulgent, lenient, conciliatory, cooperative, agreeable, tolerant, reasonable, impartial, unbiased, patient, moderate, tactful, polite, civil, kind, loyal, unselfish, helpful, sensitive, affectionate, warm, tender, sentimental, moral, honest, just, principled, sadistic, vengeful, cruel, malicious, bitter, testy, crabby, sour, surly, harsh, severe, strict, critical, bossy, derogatory, caustic, sarcastic, catty, negative, contrary, argumentative, belligerent, abrasive, unruly, aggressive, biased, opinionated, stubborn, inflexible, irritable, explosive, wild, short-tempered, jealous, mistrustful, suspicious, stingy, selfish, ungenerous, envious, scheming, sly, wily, insincere, devious, persistent, ambitious, organized, thorough, orderly, prim, tidy, discreet, controlled, serious, earnest, crusading, zealous, moralistic, prudish, predictable, rigid, conventional, rational, courtly, dignified, genteel, suave, conscientious, dependable, prompt, punctual, blasé, urbane, cultured, refined, formal, pompous, smug, proud, aimful, calculating, farseeing, progressive, mystical, devout, pious, spiritual, mature, coy, demure, chaste, unvoluptuous, economical, frugal, thrifty, unextravagant, messy, forgetful, lazy, careless, changeable, erratic, fickle, absent-minded, impolite, impudent, rude, cynical, nonreligious, informal, profane, awkward, unrefined, earthy, practical, thriftless, excessive, self-indulgent, tough, rugged, unflinching, wordless, calm, stable, sedate, peaceful, confident, independent, resourceful, ruthless, insensitive, cold, stern, frank, blunt, explicit, curt, terse, touchy, careworn, whiny, oversensitive, fearful, nervous, fussy, unstable, unconfident, self-critical, unpoised, cowardly, timid, unadventurous, wary, docile, dependent, submissive, pliant, naive, gullible, superstitious, childlike, intelligent, philosophical, complex, deep, insightful, clever, creative, curious, alert, perceptive, logical, certain, informed, literate, studious, intellectual, pensive, thoughtful, meditative, literary, poetic, artistic, musical, simple, narrow, ignorant, dull* or *illogical?*

These are all words that describe someone's personality. But, if you look closely, you can see that the words are grouped so that those with a similar meaning appear together. By grouping words together like this, you can identify underlying basic personality traits. For example, the words at the start, such as *talkative, witty, jolly, merry, lively,* could be grouped together to describe the personality trait *extrovert.* On the other hand, words like *resourceful, ruthless, insensitive* and *cold* might be grouped together to describe the personality trait *narcissist.*

Reject the dark side – head for the light triad

In fact, narcissism is one of three personality traits which have been found to be at the core of a destructive personality. Known collectively as the *Dark Triad,* they are *narcissism, Machiavellianism* and *subclinical psychopathy.*[13] These three traits overlap quite a bit, but the core of narcissism is, as we've seen, entitled self-importance, the core of Machiavellianism is manipulating other people to achieve your goals, and the core of subclinical psychopathy is lacking empathy.[14]

But recently, there has been increasing interest in the opposite of this dark side of humanity. The *Light Triad* is another group of three core traits but this time capturing the essence of a positive, rather than negative, personality.[15] The first trait of the light triad is known as *Kantianism,* and it's really the flip side of *Machiavellianism.* Kantianism involves dealing with other people without any thought of what you can get from them. It's measured with statements such as: *I don't feel comfortable overtly manipulating people to do something I want. I would like to be authentic even if it may damage my reputation. I prefer honesty over charm.*[16]

The next trait of the Light Triad is *humanism*, which involves valuing each person's dignity and worth. It's measured with statements such as: *I enjoy listening to people from all walks of life. I tend to admire others. I tend to applaud the successes of other people.*[17]

And finally, there is *faith in humanity*, which is when someone believes that humans are fundamentally good. That's measured with statements such as: *I tend to see the best in people. I tend to trust that other people will deal fairly with me. I'm quick to forgive people who have hurt me.*[18]

We all have elements of dark and light in our nature, but some people will be more consistently rooted in the *dark* traits, whilst others will be more firmly rooted in the *light* traits. What's important about the Light Triad is that it is associated with high self-esteem, good self-awareness, strong relationships, deeper spiritual experience and greater life satisfaction.[19] In short, it's really worth developing Light Triad traits. But that then raises the question: *To what degree can you change your personality?*

Can you change? Yes, you can

Way back in the 4th century BCE, the Greek philosopher Aristotle argued that our personality is not completely fixed but is shaped by our actions.[20] Two and a half thousand years later, we're beginning to get hard evidence to support this idea. For one thing, our personalities change when significant life events kick in. For example, when we get a job we love, we gradually become more conscientious – the experience changes our personality.[21] But you can't always make that kind of life event happen – what if you want to change your personality on your own?

A recent study asked participants which personality traits they would like to change in themselves. Over the course of the next 16 weeks, they were reminded of the trait or traits they had chosen to work on and were asked to come up with three goals over the course of the coming week which might help them change. They were trained to create goals which were very specific and achievable. So, a vague goal such as *be more sociable* would be turned into a specific one such as *call Andrew and ask him to lunch on Tuesday*. They were also trained in using *if..., then* goals such as *if I feel stressed, then I will call my mother to talk about it*. As they carried out these goals, week by week, their personalities started to shift.[22]

In a follow-up study the researchers developed their own pool of 50 challenges, and the participants had to choose four each week.[23] At the end of the week, if they'd achieved those challenges, they were given slightly tougher ones from the pool of 50. For example, they might start off with something like saying *hello* to a cashier in a shop and then move on to something like volunteering to take on a leadership role on a class project.[24] Again, this strategy was successful in achieving personality change. And there was a clear pattern – the more behavioural challenges that the participants successfully completed, the more their personality traits shifted over the course of the 15-week study.[25] These were not big changes – this is not like the movie where the shy nerd suddenly becomes a party animal – but still it shows that significant personality change is possible.

But there was one cautionary note. The participants who did not achieve the challenges set for them often actually displayed personality changes in the opposite direction to the one desired. In other words, if someone had said they wanted to be more extrovert and had then failed an extroversion challenge, they started to see themselves as more introverted than they had been at the start of the study.[26] So, pitching realistic, achievable challenges is really important or the whole thing can backfire.

Bringing it together with flextroversion

There's one personality trait which is associated with lots of wellbeing benefits. It's called *flextroversion*.[27] Flextroverts have three basic characteristics. Firstly, they don't rely on habits and routine behaviours but instead they act in a way that's best for each situation. A lot of our routine behaviours are performed in a kind of *autopilot* mode where we act without much conscious attention or decision-making. And that's essential because life is just too complex to give our full attention to everything that's happening to us in everyday life. But flextroverts are aware of this process and are able to come out of autopilot more easily so they can adapt their responses to new situations.[28]

Secondly, flextroverts are open to new experiences. And thirdly, flextroverts are willing to take risks to make meaningful connections with others. This might include things that make us uncomfortable, such as being the first to say *I love you* or *sorry* in a relationship, or the first to say *hello* to a stranger we're sitting next to on a train. It might involve forgiving someone or opening up to someone or being a critical friend who is not afraid to ask a difficult question.

But although these three elements of flextroversion are different, they have a common thread – the essence of being a flextrovert is being ready to do things differently in new situations. It's recognizing our unthinking, lazy, comfortable behaviours and, when they are not the right thing to do, avoiding the trap of falling back into them.

Flextroverts are better at coping with stress,[29] often because they are better at distinguishing between things they have control over and things they don't. This then means they are better at choosing the most effective strategy for dealing with a new stressful situation. And then, when they do experience stress, they are quicker to recover from it.[30] Flextroverts are less likely to be depressed[31] and less likely to be anxious.[32] They're even physically healthier[33] and better at coping with pain.[34] They're more tolerant of other people and better at coping with change.[35] With all that in mind, it's clearly worth maximizing your own flextroversion, and the good news is that it's actually not that hard to become more flextrovert.

Do something different

The key to developing flextroversion is to create small, specific behavioural challenges. In short, it's about deciding to do something different each day. This will help to nudge you out of autopilot and it will also develop your ability to remain open to new experiences – a bit like flexing a muscle so that it becomes increasingly strong.[36] The key is keeping things simple and attainable, such as:

- Take a different route to college or work.
- Watch a talk online about something you know nothing about.
- Walk down a street you've often seen but never walked down.
- Go somewhere different to buy or eat lunch.
- Listen to a song from a type of music you never usually listen to.
- Ask someone you know well to tell you something about themselves which you don't know.

- Invite someone new for a coffee.
- Buy and/or wear something you've never worn before.
- Learn a new skill, like how to do a cartwheel really well.
- Give someone you don't know well a compliment.
- Ask someone new to join your group of friends when they meet up.
- Order something to eat that you've never tried before.
- Go to a local park or landmark that you've never been to before.
- Arrange a picnic with your friends.
- Join an evening class.
- Try a night out without drinking.
- Go on a date with your boyfriend or girlfriend, pretending it's the first time you've met and you don't know anything about each other.
- Jump in a puddle.
- Spend a whole day without moaning about *anything*.

There's really no end to the behavioural challenges you could come up with in order to do something different. But make them small, achievable, very specific steps. If all of the ones above seem a little daunting, start with one inspired by a movie called *The Dead Poets Society*. In the movie an inspirational teacher encourages his students to think differently, to look at things in a new way, to seize each moment. The teacher stands on his desk and asks his students why he's up there. They can't work it out, so he tells them it's to remind himself that we must constantly look at things in a different way.[37]

This is based on a real teacher from the scriptwriter's childhood who used to teach his English class while standing on his desk, or from outside the window, or in any other different ways he could think of to make each class feel like a new experience.[38] That kept him fresh and open to new ideas and open to all of the benefits that go with being a flextrovert. So, stand up on your desk and take a look at your own room – it'll give you a whole new perspective. Then keep on doing something different.

Chapter summary

★ *Narcissists* demand your undivided attention, and your complete devotion, which can be quite seductive to start with. But soon you realize that it's suffocating.

★ Narcissism is part of the *Dark Triad*. The other two traits are *Machiavellianism* and *subclinical psychopathy*.

★ The opposite of this is the *Light Triad*, which is group of three core traits capturing the essence of a positive personality. These are *Kantianism, humanism* and *faith in humanity*.

★ *Flextroversion* is associated with lower levels of stress, depression and anxiety. Flextroverts are also physically healthier, more tolerant of other people and better at coping with change.

★ Flextroverts don't rely on habits and routine behaviours – they are *open to new experiences*, and they are *willing to take risks* to make meaningful connections with others.

★ You can become more flextrovert by challenging yourself to *do something different* each day or each week.

Take a Forest Bath

How do you feel about giving speeches? What if you've signed up to take part in an experiment and you're told that the first thing you're going to have to do is give a speech to an unknown audience?

You don't yet know what subject your speech will be about – you're going to have to make it up on the spot. The researcher then takes you to a room where there are four people sitting behind a desk at the far end. You're stood in front of a microphone and instructed to talk to them about your personal qualifications as if you were applying for a job, explaining why you are a better candidate than any other applicants. You have to keep talking like this for five minutes.

As soon as the public speaking task is finished, you're given a mental arithmetic task, still in front of the audience. You're instructed to calculate backwards, in steps of 17, from the number 2043: *2043, 2026, 2009, 1992…* Every time you make a mistake, you're told to start again, from 2043.

By this point, you're probably feeling pretty stressed. Of course, that's the point. This procedure is called the *Trier Social Stress Test (TSST)* and it's designed to activate both of your biological stress response systems[1] – that is, the immediate *fight-or-flight* system, and the longer-term chronic stress system, which is called the *HPA axis*. What this means is that, after the public speaking and mental arithmetic tasks, you'll be releasing significantly higher levels of cortisol and your heart will be pumping.

Rippling water and flowering meadows

This test is used to find the best ways to cope with stress. For example, a group of participants who spent ten minutes listening to the sound of rippling water before undergoing the TSST had significantly lower cortisol levels throughout and after the test than other people who had simply rested for ten minutes.[2] The sound of rippling water was more effective in reducing stress than relaxing music. In other words, it was something about the *naturalness* of the sound which was relaxing.

But it's not just *listening* to nature which works – *looking* at nature is also surprisingly good for you. For example, just taking a 40-second micro-break to look at a flowering meadow scene boosted students' ability to focus and sustain their attention.[3] And this is not just mental – it's physical too, because having a view of a natural landscape from your hospital bed seems to improve recovery after surgery.[4]

Getting closer with pot plants

With all that good stuff going on just by listening and looking at nature, what happens when you get your hands dirty with some real, live direct contact? Well, it doesn't take much – even small amounts of nature contact seem to be very beneficial. For example, after just 15 minutes of transplanting pot plants in a greenhouse, participants in one study reported feeling significantly more relaxed than they did after 15 minutes of a computer task. This finding was backed up by the fact that their blood pressure was significantly lower after the transplanting task.[5]

When 503 office staff at an American university were asked about the amount of contact they had with nature at work, similar results were found. The researchers asked about things like whether the office workers took breaks outdoors, whether they had a view from their desk, and the number of pot plants in the office. They found that the more contact people had with nature, the less stressed they felt and the fewer general health complaints they reported.[6]

Full immersion with *shinrin-yoku*

So, gentle contact with nature certainly seems to be good, but it turns out that taking a full-on bath in an anti-rotting agent makes you feel great! We're talking here about *phytoncides* – the airborne chemicals that many plants and trees emit to prevent them from rotting or being eaten by insects and animals.[7] In fact, immersing yourself in them is so popular in Japan that it has its own name: *shinrin-yoku*. This literally means *forest bath*, and that's how the Japanese see the whole experience – like a deep, relaxing bath where you immerse yourself not in water but in the whole experience of being in a forest.

Phytoncides have been found to reduce blood pressure and boost your immune system.[8] And there's mounting evidence that simply being in a forest has a massive range of health benefits, both physical and mental. For example, taking a day off to walk in a forest is better at reducing stress than taking a day off to engage in your favourite activities or carry out physical exercise. It's something about the forest which is reducing stress – not the time off, not engaging in favourite activities, not the exercise. It's the shinrin-yoku. Even better, the researchers also found that the length of time in the forest did not affect the results, so a short forest bath seems to be enough to seriously drop the stress levels.[9,10,11]

You don't need to find yourself an ancient forest in the middle of nowhere to get these effects. A study on 1,538 people living Brisbane, Australia, found that the people who were spending the longest amount of time in any kind of nature experience, such as walking in a park, were significantly less likely to have depression and high blood pressure.[12]

This is not about hiking

When you stack up all the mental and physical benefits of contact with nature, it's pretty much jaw-dropping. Among other things, you find that it helps with depression, anxiety, diabetes, attention deficit hyperactivity disorder (ADHD), cancer, healing from surgery, obesity, birth outcomes, cardiovascular disease, musculoskeletal complaints, migraines, respiratory disease, stress and even life expectancy.[13] In short, it's good for you – *really good* – but why?

One idea was that contact with nature must mean getting exercise – like hiking through a forest – and that it's the *exercise* which is really giving you the benefit. But this doesn't stack up with the evidence. The health benefits of contact with nature hold up regardless of the amount of exercise people take. For example, people who live in areas with lots of green spaces do not consistently display higher levels of exercise, and yet they do consistently display lower rates of obesity.[14] If that seems like an odd finding, keep in mind that we've already seen the powerful way in which contact with nature reduces stress. So, it may well be that the reduced stress leads to less eating and so less obesity. In fact, nature contact also increases your ability to resist acting on impulse. This is also likely to reduce obesity by reducing impulsive eating.[15]

Another theory is that contact with nature inevitably leads to contact with other people and so it's this social support which is giving you the benefit. Of course, spending time with other people is great, but it's not what's driving these amazing benefits of contact with nature. We know that because we've already seen how just listening to natural sounds or looking at a view is enough for the benefits to kick in, even in laboratory settings.

You were not formed in an office

So, this is not about hiking, and it's not about meeting up with people. Firstly, it's about the biochemical environment. Not only are there the phytoncides which boost immune functioning, but there are also high concentrations of negative air ions in forests,[16] which have a variety of beneficial effects, including reducing depression.[17]

Secondly, it's something to do with our evolutionary past. Our brains and bodies have been shaped not by offices or lecture halls but by forests and mountains, rivers and lakes, beaches and cliffs. What this means is that the sights and sounds of these natural experiences are hard-wired into us. When we're detached from them, something in us realizes that we're in an unnatural state – the body senses that all is not quite as it should be, so our stress responses are more easily triggered. Reverse that – allow the sights and sounds and textures of nature back into our lives – and our brain senses that all is well, that it can come off alert mode and tune down the stress response systems.[18]

But there's an even more immediate reason why this is not about hiking purposefully though a forest, navigating from A to B as quickly as you can. Most of our lives are dominated by this kind of mind-set, by the ideal of being productive, multi-tasking and getting things done. But when you're in a forest, you can't get it *done*. And that often means that time slows down and it's easier just to be in the moment rather than constantly looking ahead at a deadline. This is what shinrin-yoku is all about. It's the opposite of hiking. The idea is to allow yourself the time and space to walk slowly in the forest, without any particular goal or destination.[19] This way you can connect with the forest with all of your senses: listening to the birds and the wind in the leaves, looking at the shades of green and the shapes of the branches, taking in those phytoncides, touching the rough bark of the trees as you feel a breeze on your face. This is shinrin-yoku, and there is some real, hard science behind it.

Chapter summary

★ Listening to the sound of rippling water is more effective for reducing stress than relaxing music. It's something about the *naturalness* of the sound which is relaxing.

★ Looking at a natural view increases our ability to maintain *focused attention* and *speeds up recovery* from illness.

★ *Phytoncides* have been found to reduce blood pressure and boost your immune system.

★ Immersing yourself in phytoncides is so popular in Japan that it has its own name: *shinrin-yoku*. This literally means *forest bath*.

★ Any kind of nature experience, such as walking in a park, significantly reduces your likelihood of *depression* and *high blood pressure*.

★ There are three main reasons, that we know of so far, as to why nature contact makes us feel better – the *phytoncides*, the fact that *our brains were built to be in nature*, and the fact that nature contact slows us down and *helps us to notice the present moment.*

Do (Almost) Nothing

What if there was a simple way of hacking into the most creative parts of your mind?

The man who invented the lightbulb certainly thought there was. His name was Thomas Edison and he would sit in a chair holding a steel ball in one hand. On the floor under this hand was a metal saucepan. He would allow himself to relax completely while he considered a problem he was struggling with. Gradually he would begin to drift off but, just as he was falling asleep, his hand would relax and drop the steel ball onto the pan, waking him up.

There was always a pencil and paper kept close at hand with which he would quickly write down all the ideas that had come to him in that state of consciousness somewhere between awake and asleep. His secret was that fully conscious thought can take you almost all the way to solving a problem, but the relaxed state of mind, just as you enter sleep, is necessary to reach the true moments of genius. That's why he called this technique the *genius gap*.[1] And it seems to have worked. This is the man who was perhaps the most prolific inventor in history, with at least 1,093 original ideas formally recorded during his lifetime – each one representing a moment of creative invention.[2]

The *Fluid Interfaces Group* at the Massachusetts Institute of Technology (MIT) have developed a device called *Dormio* which is bringing the steel ball trick up to date with cutting-edge technology.[3] It's a hand-worn sleep stage tracker which can detect when you are somewhere between wakefulness and sleep. The technical term for this state of consciousness is *hypnagogia*. Dormio keeps you in hypnagogia by using sound that's loud enough to stop you from going into deeper sleep but not loud enough to fully wake you. It's a bit like Edison's steel ball dropping onto a soft surface rather than a metal pan, so that the ball lands with a dampened thud just loud enough to stop you dropping off into deep sleep but not loud enough to fully wake you. The people who have tried it describe the experience as a bit like thinking in the third person – as though they are slightly outside of their own thoughts, observing them.[4]

Doing nothing is harder than it looks

You don't need technology to hack into the creative areas of your mind. Isaac Newton, for example, is said to have been sitting under a tree when the *law of gravity* came to him.[5] This momentous idea '...was occasion'd by the fall of an apple, as he sat in contemplative mood.'[6] In other words, doing nothing can also help you to access your own creativity.

The thing is, focusing on a task is like training a narrow spotlight onto a single point. This is really useful for many tasks that require thinking about one or two things at a time. But mind wandering is like turning on a bare lightbulb in a cluttered attic, revealing all kinds of unrelated things. The mind wanders widely across apparently unrelated thoughts, looking for strange and interesting connections.[7] And it's these connections which lead to creative ideas.

But there's a catch. It's not that easy to do nothing. In fact, researchers from the University of Virginia found that most people can't do it at all. The people in this study were put into a room and told to entertain themselves with their thoughts – essentially to let their mind wander. There was nothing in the room except for a button which, if they really wanted to distract themselves from their own thoughts, they could press to give themselves a mild electric shock. They had already experienced the shock and they had all said they would *pay money* not to experience it again. And yet 67% of the men and 25% of the women shocked themselves in order to avoid being left alone with...themselves.[8]

The thing is, mind wandering is not effortless. Think about it – when you're exhausted and you just want to flop down and veg out, you don't tend to do *nothing*. You're more likely to put on a trashy film, or flick through multiple TV programmes, or scroll through Instagram posts, or even press a nearby button which you know will give you a mild electric shock. Doing nothing at all, letting your mind wander, actually requires effort.

Doing nothing can be dangerous

As well as the effort it takes, there's a further problem with doing nothing – sometimes your mind uses that time to *ruminate*.[9] This involves repeatedly going over the same negative thoughts. For example: *What am I doing to deserve this? Why do I always react this way? Why do I have problems other people don't have? Why can't I handle things better?*[10] What's interesting about rumination is that it feels like a form of mind wandering, but it actually requires *focus*.

Your mind is using the freedom of doing nothing to focus on the same negative thoughts and emotions time and again.

So, in order to get the most benefit from mind wandering, we need to get a balance – we need to do something that gives our mind enough focus so that it can't ruminate, but make that thing we're doing simple enough that there's space for our minds to wander. We need a hack that maximizes the benefits of unfocused creative mind wandering whilst minimizing the risk of focused ruminating. In fact, the hack is pretty straightforward – you have to do *almost* nothing.

Doing just the right amount of nothing

Here's how we know that doing almost nothing works. A recent study used the *Unusual Uses Task (UUT)* to measure creative thinking.[11] This is where you're shown an everyday object (such as a brick) and you have two minutes to come up with as many unusual uses for it as you can. You're scored on the originality and number of uses you come up with for each object you're shown. The researchers found that, when people were given an *undemanding task* for 12 minutes before the creative thinking test, they were much more creative than other people who were allowed simply to sit and do nothing at all before the test.

It seems that creative thinking and creative problem-solving happens most effectively when you're doing an undemanding task. There are two main reasons for this. The first, as we've already seen, is that the undemanding task stops the focused thought that allows rumination, but it leaves enough of the mind's resources free for plenty of creative mind wandering. The second reason is that this kind of undemanding task occupies just enough of the mind's attention to stop the desire to reach for a distraction. That means you can remain in the mind wandering state for longer. There's a Goldilocks element to this – not too much freedom, not too little freedom – the undemanding task allows your mind *just the right* amount of freedom to wander creatively for extended periods of time.

How to do almost nothing

Let's make one thing really clear – picking up your phone is not an undemanding task. It demands attention and obliterates mind wandering. The undemanding task in the study above involved a computer generating coloured numbers and asking the participants to indicate whether they were odd or even. These coloured numbers would appear infrequently, allowing plenty of time for the mind to wander even though the participants had to stay on task. This is not very practical in everyday life, but there are a range of undemanding tasks which can work just as well and are easier to set up.

For example, doodling or aimless drawing does everything needed for creative mind wandering. It takes up enough attention to prevent focused, goal-directed thought, it leaves enough space for the mind to wander, and it prevents negative feelings of boredom so that you are less likely to reach for a distraction. That makes it *just* undemanding enough to allow you to remain suspended in a state of undirected, creative mind wandering.[12] The recent explosion in the sales of adult colouring books becomes more understandable here because this is a similar kind of undemanding task which fits the creative mind wandering requirements. Crafts such as knitting or crocheting would also fit, as would many household chores, such as gardening or washing-up.

Sometimes the undemanding task might be set up for you.

For example, sitting on a bus or a train, watching the world go by, is just undemanding enough to free up the mind for creative thought. Often, we use these moments to catch up on emails and social media, but it's worth putting the phone down and seeing what kind of ideas float to the surface.

A more active alternative is walking or cycling. This can be either outside or in a gym – because either of these situations really does increase creativity.[13] What's important is that the walk should be open-ended and not goal-directed. That means not walking to try to get somewhere by a certain time or setting distance targets on the treadmill. It's the *process* which is important here – the experience of the undemanding task must be enough to satisfy the mind, without any need to look ahead to a finished outcome or product. In addition, it's often more effective if the undemanding task is a physical activity, as this tends to have the further benefit of being calming. Being calm is important for the kind of relaxed thought that, as we have already seen, lies behind creativity.[14]

Should you care about doing almost nothing?

I think you should, and I think a look at the underlying neuroscience is the best way to explain why. Neuroscience is unfolding a fascinating story about the downtime of unfocused brain activity. It started with the discovery of the brain's *default mode*. That's a system of interconnected brain structures which become active when we're not focused on a particular task.[15] It's the brain in its resting state, except it isn't resting at all – it's really busy in creative thought.[16] C.S. Lewis, who wrote the Narnia stories, puts it like this: 'I am the product of long corridors, empty sunlit rooms, upstair indoor silences...'[17]

So, yes, doing almost nothing in order to activate the default mode – that's important. But that's not all. Doing almost nothing is also central to our sense of identity. This is because it's when we're using the brain's default mode that we tell ourselves stories about who we think we are. As our minds wander, we go over things that have happened to us in the past and we imagine things that might happen in the future. We start to see ourselves more clearly as the central character in this ongoing story. All the while, we're thinking about how other people see us, and predicting how other people will act in a certain situation.

Making time to let this happen is important in developing your sense of identity. You need time to work out who you are and where you fit in your social world. In fact, many psychologists have argued that developing a clear sense of identity is the *most* important task of adolescence and young adulthood.[18] If you don't take the time to do almost nothing, you are giving up an incredibly valuable opportunity to develop your sense of identity. Not fully exploring your sense of identity can have a negative effect on your sense of purpose and meaning in life, your ability to develop intimate relationships and your wellbeing.[19]

So, if there are likely to be problems in your life which need creative solutions, and if you think it's important to have meaning, purpose and identity, then take some time to do almost nothing.

Chapter summary

★ A number of creative geniuses have used *hypnagogia* – a state of consciousness somewhere between wakefulness and sleep – to solve problems. This is because the unfocused mind can be more creative.

★ Doing nothing at all can lead to *rumination*, which is actually a focused state and so will not lead to creativity.

★ To maximize the opportunities of creative mind wandering, you need to use an *undemanding task* which provides enough focus to stop rumination but enough freedom to allow for creative mind wandering. In other words, you need to do *almost* nothing.

★ Undemanding tasks should be *open-ended* (not goal-directed) and ideally *physical*, such as aimless drawing or walking.

★ Doing almost nothing activates the brain's *default mode*, which, as well as driving creativity, is important for developing meaning, purpose and identity.

Take an Exercise Snack

Even a short walk of just a few minutes improves how we feel. This is called an exercise snack because it's quick, easy and you can do it almost anywhere.

What's really interesting about *exercise snacks* is that it's exactly *because* they're short that they work so well. This is because it's the changing from one state to another – from sitting still to walking, to sitting still again – that gives us the boost.[1]

And it's not just about feeling good – these small changes in physical activity lead to big gains in creative thinking. That's because it's the first few minutes of physical activity when you're at your most creative.[2] Then, when you stop walking, and return to your desk, that change gives you another creative boost.[3] It's not often you hear that sitting back down is good for you. But it is, as long as you've done a small bit of moving around beforehand.

It's not going to be practical to spend the whole day taking five minutes on and five minutes off, but having some kind of change at least every hour certainly does seem to work on both wellbeing and creativity. And there are lots of ways you can use these ideas in everyday life to take frequent exercise snacks. You can choose the stairs rather than taking an elevator.[4] If you walk to the bus stop, you could stop every few minutes and take a look at your surroundings – to get that physical change needed for creativity.[5] If you're working at a desk, stand up and move at least every half an hour.[6] And to help that process you could set up cues to remind you, like standing up every time you open up a new email or take a sip of coffee. The options are pretty much endless, but the important thing is to look out for opportunities to take an exercise snack and gradually build them into your day.

If the idea of walking seems too boring, then put on your favourite track and dance around your room for five minutes. Humans have been dancing for so long that it's built into our DNA. That means you can use it to access a range of biological benefits. For example, it will have an immediate effect on your mood, which can be directly measured through hormonal changes. You can also get a creative thinking boost, by improvising – just dance around the room, making it up as you go along.[7]

Turning it up a level

When you're a *Formula One* mechanic, your car is always evolving. It's built, stripped back, and rebuilt to fit new parts that might improve its speed by hundredths of a second. Then, during the race, your team is constantly assessing the track conditions – fitting and re-fitting different types of tyres to keep the car at optimum performance.

The thing is, there are *mechanics* just like this in your body. They're called *BDNF proteins*, and the machine they're working on is your brain. They're strengthening key connections between brain cells, building new connections, and getting rid of connections that are not currently useful.[8] The technical term for this whole process is *activity dependent neural plasticity*. That just means physically shaping and reshaping your brain to keep it at optimum performance. This is what helps you cope with new, challenging situations, just like changing tyres to adapt to new track conditions.[9]

So, when you have plenty of *BDNF mechanics* working on your brain, you're less likely to experience depression.[10] We know this because people suffering from depression typically have low levels of BDNF.[11] Even anti-depressant drugs, which were thought to work by increasing neurotransmitters such as *serotonin*, are now thought to work by increasing levels of BDNF.[12]

How do I get more BDNF mechanics working on my brain?

Here's the great news – exercise boosts your levels of BDNF, even after a single session.[13, 14] And that's why it's increasingly used as a treatment, not only for depression[15] but also for anxiety,[16] regardless of your age and health.[17] Specifically, it's *anaerobic* exercise which is great for boosting BDNF – that's the more intense physical activity, such as weight-lifting or sprinting.[18] And a particularly effective form of anaerobic exercise is *high intensity interval training (HIIT)*.[19]

HIIT involves short bursts of vigorous activity, performed at maximum effort.[20] And short really does mean short – it's probably going to be about 20–30 *seconds* of maximum effort,[21] certainly not more than a minute. The important thing is to go at it right up until your body just can't do it anymore. That might mean feeling muscle burn or getting to a point when it would be difficult to carry out a conversation with someone because you're so out of breath. Then you rest for a few seconds up to about four minutes, depending on your fitness level. The important thing is that your rest is just long enough to allow you to do another 100% effort burst of exercise.[22] Repeat that 4–6 times,[23] so that the whole session should last less than 20 minutes, including warm-up and cool-down stages.

This doesn't require a gym or any equipment, because you can use whole-body exercises. For beginners, the recommendation is to keep it simple with exercises like jumping jacks, squats, push-ups, crunches, lunges, or simply running on the spot. If you're generally fitter, more complex exercises like burpees or single-leg deadlifts might be better.[24]

Obviously, when you're starting out on something like this, you need to build it up slowly so that each time you push it a little harder you can check that your body is able to tolerate the stress you're putting it under.[25] Also, this type of training should not be carried out every day as pushing your body so hard means that you need time to recover – to rest and repair in preparation for the next session. So, something like three times per week is the maximum.[26] That's a time commitment of around one hour a week to boost your BDNF levels significantly, which, in turn, will help to stop depression or anxiety.[27]

What exercise and cannabis have in common

(Warning – more technical terminology coming up)

So, we know that you can boost BDNF, but it doesn't stop there. There's something else that exercise can do for your brain and it has to do with *endocannabinoids*. Did you know that you have an *endocannabinoid system* in your body?[28] If not, don't worry – neither did anyone else right up until the 1990s. You may have noticed, from its name, that it has something to do with cannabis. The link is that *THC*, the active component of cannabis, produces its effect by disrupting this system.

The endocannabinoid system works by using two main endocannabinoids – these are molecules which happen to be called *AEA* and *2-AG*.[29] When you boost the levels of the AEA endocannabinoid, you can get results which are similar to taking anti-anxiety medication (at least in rats).[30] And when you reduce levels of the 2-AG endocannabinoid, it increases levels of anxiety (at least in mice).[31] If you're not impressed by all these animal study findings, one minute with someone who has voluntarily activated their endocannabinoid system (by getting stoned) will show you that the effect is to make that person pretty relaxed.[32] The problem with this kind of self-medication by taking cannabis is that it comes with all kinds of side effects.[33] Endocannabinoids, on the other hand, are produced naturally by the body and have no such drawbacks.

Related to this, the endocannabinoid system in your body also has a direct effect on your stress response. When you experience something stressful, you produce endocannabinoids, which reduce the experience of anxiety. Specifically, AEA seems to keep a check on the intensity of your biological stress response, whereas 2-AG calms your body down after a stressful event, bringing everything back to normal.[34]

What's even better is that your body's endocannabinoid system learns from experience and produces increasingly high levels of endocannabinoids if you keep on experiencing the same stressful event repeatedly. This means you become increasingly effective at dealing with it calmly.[35] And, as if all that isn't enough, endocannabinoids are used for memory. They actually help to prevent the formation and retrieval of traumatic memories.[36,37]

I need all that good stuff – can I get more endocannabinoids?

Well, yes you can. It costs nothing. And it takes three minutes. Three minutes of *isometric* exercise increases the levels of both endocannabinoids: AEA and 2-AG.[38] Isometric exercise is where you don't move – you get into a static position which puts some strain on your muscles and you hold it for as long as you can. For example, getting into a push-up position but, rather than doing push-ups, you simply hold your body weight. This can be pretty strenuous so, just as with HIIT, you need to build it up slowly and avoid holding your breath or putting excess strain on your body, especially if you have high blood pressure.[39]

If that sounds a little too intense, moderate levels of exercise have been found to increase levels of circulating endocannabinoids.[40] To give you an idea of what it looks like, moderate exercise is very brisk walking, heavy-duty cleaning (washing windows or vacuuming), mowing the lawn, light-effort bicycling (10–12mph), recreational badminton and tennis doubles.[41] A single session of moderate exercise for 30 minutes is enough to significantly increase the AEA endocannabinoid and get what's sometimes called a *runner's high*.[42]

BDNF or endocannabinoids – how about both?

You don't need to choose between a BDNF boost or extra endocannabinoids, as it looks like there's a link between them anyway. For example, when you measure both AEA and BDNF during exercise you find a positive correlation – as the level of one of them goes up, so does the other.[43] And it seems as though it's the increasing level of endocannabinoids which causes the increase in BDNF. In other words, exercise increases endocannabinoids and these then increase BDNF.[44]

What we do and don't know

Given the massive variety of exercise programmes and the different levels of fitness that each person has, it's perhaps not surprising that there's still a lot we don't know about the link between exercise and wellbeing. But – here's what we *do* know.

We know that the more physical activity you do, the less likely you are to be diagnosed with depression. It's a fact that physical activity protects you from feeling depressed.[45] We also know that exercise is free and comes without any of the side effects that you risk with medication. And we know that you can choose almost any level of physical activity, from a five-minute walk to a 20-minute HIIT workout. Whatever the level, it will still give you a wellbeing boost.

Finally, we know from research that the benefits of exercise are not due to the *placebo effect*. The placebo effect is when you feel better only because you *believe* that a treatment will make you feel better. The problem with that is that the treatment itself is doing nothing, so as soon as your belief in it starts to fail, so do the positive effects. Exercise is different. Even if you're sceptical and you don't think it will make you feel better – it will.[46] The problem is that sometimes, when you're down, the last thing you want to do is get up and move. But you have to ignore the voice that might be telling you it's a waste of time, or that you can't be bothered. All it takes is a few minutes. All it takes is an exercise snack.

Chapter summary

★ Even short walks of just a few minutes improve how we feel and make us more creative. It's not so much the physical activity but *the change of state* – from sitting still to walking – which is effective.

★ There are *BDNF proteins* in your brain. They're like *Formula One* car mechanics, constantly working to keep your brain running at optimal performance.

★ You can boost your own levels of BDNF by using *high intensity interval training (HIIT)*. This involves 4–6 short bursts of vigorous activity, followed by rest periods of around four minutes.

★ You also have an *endocannabinoid system* in your body which helps to reduce anxiety and deal with stress. You can boost your *endocannabinoids* by doing 3 minutes of *isometric exercise* or 30 minutes of moderate exercise.

Breathe Tactically

'Everything went black. I thought I was dead. It was very serene, peaceful, and calm. Then, the worst pain imaginable seized my body. The deafening noise of my skull shattering forced me to open my eyes. All I could see was bright light, eerily like "the light" of near-death experience. I couldn't make anything out. I knew the only thing that could hurt this badly was that I had just been shot.'

These are the words of Tricia Kennedy, a police officer who had just been shot accidently during a shooting competition.[1] A round from a .45 Remington Full Metal Jacket had broken through the barrier of a nearby range and hit her in the head. By this time, she was hyperventilating, convulsing and sliding into unconsciousness. Then she heard someone say, 'You must breathe – you're going into shock, and we're going to lose you.'

Those words triggered something in her mind. She remembered a training exercise where she and her fellow officers had been taught to breathe. You might think: *Why does anyone need to be taught how to breathe? We all know how to breathe, otherwise we'd be dead.* And that's true, but breathing is special. It is an automatic response – like our heartbeat – but the difference is that breathing can also be *consciously controlled*.[2] We can control breathing to play wind instruments, or to shout, or sing. We can also decide to speed it up or slow it down. That's why Tricia had received the training. She had been taught something called *combat breathing*. This is a breathing technique designed to keep you calm in situations of intense pressure; because the control you have over breathing gives you control over other things, such as stress and panic. That's what makes it so amazing, and that's why knowing how to breathe saved Tricia's life.

Catching your breath

But there's more to breathing than keeping calm. Breathing affects almost everything we do. For example, imagine you're in a room with a group of strangers. It's the first day of a new course and you're all sitting around a large conference table, waiting for the tutor to come in and start things off. No one has spoken yet, but somehow you can tell who the most confident person in the room is. The thing is, you don't know what it is about them that's giving that impression.

Then, a discussion starts up and you immediately sense that this person is calm and controlled. Their voice is not loud but, when they speak, everyone stops to listen. It's clear and resonant. This person may not even know the secret of their own confidence, but it's linked to breath. The most confident person in the room will be the one who is breathing the slowest and the deepest.[3]

Suddenly, someone turns to you and asks your opinion. Your brain goes into overdrive trying to work out an answer as quickly as possible so as not to look like an idiot. But what about your breathing? Do you *catch your breath*? Do you stop breathing, just for a moment, while you work out what to say? If so, you wouldn't be alone – many people hold their breath when concentrating. Even something as simple as texting can make people hold their breath.[4] And, after you do, there's a pattern of quick, shallow breaths to catch up.

The problem with this is that quick, shallow breathing is exactly what happens when your sympathetic nervous system – the *fight or flight* response – is activated. This fight or flight system evolved to get you out of physical dangers such as being attacked by an animal. In dangerous situations, it's doing everything right. It's increasing your heart rate and blood pressure – sending extra blood to the muscles so that you're pumped and ready for action. It quickens your breath, drawing in the oxygen that your brain and muscles need.

But the same response can happen just because someone unexpectedly asks you to speak in front of a group of strangers. Your body doesn't know the difference – tiger, falling tree, public speaking, working right up to a deadline, argument with your partner, a disturbing thought – they all trigger the same stress response. But when the fight or flight response kicks in for something which doesn't actually require us to run away or fight, it feels like anxiety and stress. And we can be triggering this response many times a day without even realizing it.

Once a threat has passed, a different system in your body kicks in. This is called the *parasympathetic system* and it's there to calm you down and return you to normal. By purposefully slowing down your breathing, you can override the fight or flight response and activate this calming system.[5] In other words, just by consciously slowing down your breathing you can reduce your heart rate, blood pressure and stress-related cortisol levels.[6,7] It's a bit like tricking your body into assuming that everything is now okay, even if your mind is still stressed and scared. And when your body calms down, your emotions will follow – stress and anxiety will drop.[8]

How to breathe

Using your diaphragm

Put the palm of one hand on your chest and the palm of the other hand on your belly. Now take a breath but try to expand only your chest, so only the chest-hand moves outwards. What you are doing is using your *intercostal muscles* to breathe. These are the muscles that run in-between your ribs.

Now try another breath, but this time try to expand only your belly, so that only your belly-hand moves outwards. This time you're using your *diaphragm*. This is a thin muscle, shaped like a parachute, that lies right under your lungs. And it's *this* kind of breathing – using your diaphragm – which is best. Basically, breathing like this is always slower and deeper than chest breathing, so it's linked to all the benefits mentioned above (e.g. reduced anxiety and increased focus).

To really get a sense of it, press your thumbs gently into your abdomen just below your rib cage. As you breathe in, you should feel your thumbs being pushed outwards. Then, as you breathe out, you should feel them moving back inwards. That's your diaphragm pushing against your thumbs. And that's the source of good, calm, confident breathing. Another way of feeling the power of the diaphragm is to put your hands on your side ribs so your elbows are sticking out. As you inhale, make your ribs go out to the side. Then relax and let your ribs move back to where they were at rest.

Your nose is awesome #1: *It slows down breathing*

An even simpler way to slow down your breathing is to breathe through your nose. That's because, when you inhale through your nose, there's more resistance, so you just can't take in your breath as quickly as you can through the mouth. The slower breathing activates the parasympathetic nervous system, bringing with it all the calming, anti-stress, anti-anxiety effects.

Your nose is awesome #2: *It helps recall*

Breathing through your nose improves your memory.[9] It's something to do with the fact that we use breathing to help us focus.[10] For example, pianists unconsciously align their breathing to the rhythm of the music they are thinking about.[11] But breathing also affects a part of your brain called the *hippocampus,* which is central to long-term memory function. Breathing through your nose activates the *olfactory bulb,* which in turn activates the *piriform cortex,* which in turn boosts the hippocampus.[12] This amazing process is lost when you bypass your nose and breathe through your mouth.

Your nose is awesome #3: *More amazing nose facts*

- It warms, humidifies and cleans the air, preparing it for the lungs.
- It regulates the direction and speed of the air stream to maximize exposure to a network of fine arteries, veins, lymphatics and nerves.
- It boosts the inhalation of nitric oxide, which increases your ability to transport oxygen throughout the body.
- It traps large particles with the nose hairs and small particles via mucous membrane.
- It helps to prevent colds, flu, allergic reaction, hay fever and irritable coughing.
- It helps to ensure the correct position of the tongue (against the upper palate) and lips (together), making correct formation of the natural dental arches and straight teeth more likely.
- It reduces the likelihood of snoring and apnoea (sleep disturbance).

Tactical breathing

Once you have the basics of breathing, you can use different breathing patterns for different experiences.

Combat breathing

This simple technique is used by the police and military to regain or keep control in a highly stressful situation.[13] This is the technique which effectively saved Tricia Kennedy's life. It has a *4-4-4-4* structure which works like this:

1. Inhale through your nose as you count to 4.
2. Hold the air in your lungs for a count of 4. Do not clamp down and create pressure – just maintain an expansive, open feeling even though you are not inhaling.
3. Exhale as you count to 4.
4. Wait for a count of 4.
5. Repeat.

4-7-8 breathing

This technique, developed by Andrew Weil, M.D.,[14] is for deep relaxation. That makes it ideal for de-stressing or for getting off to sleep, but you can also use it to see off an unwanted craving. This one has a *4-7-8* structure, but keep in mind that the 4, 7 and 8 are not seconds but steady counts. It's the pattern of each breath rather than how long you breathe in/out for. That's important because you should make sure the counts are quick enough so that you don't feel uncomfortable and out of breath at any point. This is how it works:

1. Inhale through your nose while counting to 4.
2. Hold the air in your lungs for a count of 7. Again, do not

clamp down and create pressure – just maintain an expansive, open feeling even though you are not inhaling.

3. Exhale from your mouth for a count of 8.
4. Repeat.

Coffee breathing

This is the opposite of the two techniques above. It's designed to give you a burst of energy by activating your fight or flight system, so it's a bit like a strong coffee. And just like strong coffee, it should be used very sparingly. Three rounds of 20 breaths at about 3pm is useful as this is when your cortisol levels drop, which can leave you feeling drowsy. Coffee breathing, rather than actual coffee, is a natural way to re-set your body to alertness.[15] Just follow these steps:

1. Focus on the exhale only – allow the inhale to happen automatically.
2. Exhale through your nose 20 times in sharp, shooting breaths, like a sneeze, or like you're trying to shift something out of your nostrils in sharp bursts.
3. Try not to move your face, shoulders or chest – the bursts of breath should come from your lower abdomen.

Breath counting

This is slightly different in that it's not meant to change the way you breathe but instead it's designed to help you become more *aware* of your breathing. If you find yourself worrying a lot about something that's happened in the past or about something that might happen in the future, this can really help to bring you gently into the present moment. It's often useful for getting off to sleep. Here's what to do:

1. Put one hand on your chest and the other hand on your

belly. Then, focus on breathing slowly with your tummy, so that the chest hand doesn't move very much.

2. Breathing slowly like this, simply say the number *one* to yourself as you exhale.
3. The next time you exhale, say the number *two* to yourself.
4. On the third exhale, say the number *three*.
5. On the fourth exhale, say the number *four*.
6. On the fifth exhale, say the number *five*.
7. After the fifth exhale, start again at one and keep repeating the cycle.

The great thing about only counting up to five is that you can tell when your mind has wandered back onto those worries because you'll suddenly realize that, rather than starting again after the fifth exhale, you're counting out your ninth or even nineteenth exhale. When that happens, don't stress or beat yourself up, simply draw yourself back to the exercise, starting again from one. About ten minutes of this can really help to see off the anxiety which worrying about the past or the future can create.

Wim Hof breathing

Wim Hof is a Dutch extreme athlete – known as *The Iceman* – who walked to the top of Mount Kilimanjaro wearing only shorts.[16] He developed this breathing technique to induce a short-term stress response which ultimately can lead to more resilience towards everyday stresses. But with all that in mind, you'll see that this is not for the fainthearted and should be used with caution.

Especially important is that you should NEVER do this breathing exercise in a swimming pool, before going underwater, in the shower or piloting any vehicle. Always do it in a safe environment – lying down or sitting comfortably. And don't force it – build up gradually, keeping well within your own comfort zone and limits.

One round goes like this:

1. Breathe in fully with both your diaphragm and your chest.
2. Let go of the breath – don't force the air out fully – just let the breath go till you are relaxed.
3. Do that about 30 times.
4. Then hold your breath for as long as is comfortable (usually 1–2 minutes or so).
5. When you feel the urge to take a breath, breathe in deeply and hold it for about 10 seconds.
6. Breathe out.
7. Do 3–4 rounds on an empty stomach, ideally first thing in the morning.

...and breathe

The formal word for breathing – *respiration* – comes from the word *spirit*, which means to give life. That's why, in Christianity, it's the *Spirit of God* which forms the Earth and it's through the *Holy Spirit* that the Virgin Mary becomes pregnant with Jesus Christ. There's more of this mystery in the word *inspiration* – it not only means to draw air into the lungs but also has an older meaning to suggest a *divine influence*. You can still hear this older meaning when someone is said to have given an *inspirational performance*, like some higher presence took them over and lifted their performance to a new level.

It's not surprising that, for millennia, breath, life and spirituality have been linked. You can live for over three weeks without food. You can survive for a little over three days without water. But, if you stop breathing, you'll be struggling to survive after about three minutes. So, in a very direct kind of way, breath is life. That makes it all the more amazing that you can hack into your breathing and use it tactically to improve your life.

Chapter summary

★ Breathing is an *automatic response* – like our heartbeat – but it can also be *consciously controlled*.

★ Quick, shallow breathing activates your *fight or flight* response. We can be triggering this response many times a day without even realizing it.

★ By purposefully slowing down your breathing, you can override the fight or flight response and activate the *parasympathetic system* which calms you down.

★ Breathing with your belly uses a muscle called the *diaphragm*, and this kind of breathing is good because it's slower and deeper than chest breathing.

★ There are lots of benefits of breathing through your nose. For example, it slows down your breathing and helps you focus.

★ *Combat breathing, 4-7-8 breathing, coffee breathing, breath counting* and *Wim Hof breathing* are all powerful ways you can use breathing tactically to improve your life.

CONNECT

Verb / kəˈnekt
to bring people together

Stop Liking People

On 3 September 1833 something happened which was so important that the design of your phone, nearly 200 years later, can be traced back to it.

A man called Benjamin Day started publishing a newspaper called *The New York Sun*. What was different was that he was selling his newspaper for one penny, a price that was guaranteed to make a loss. This didn't matter to him because the people buying the paper were not his customers – they were his product. He was going to sell their attention to businesses throughout New York. Why was their attention profitable? Because once you had someone's attention, you could sell them stuff.

Benjamin Day needed a lot of people to buy his newspaper before their combined attention was going to be worth the serious money he intended to make. And he had two secret weapons. The first was the price – he was practically giving away the newspaper. The second was the headlines. Using perhaps the first examples of what we now call *clickbait* and *fake news*, he was a pioneer of headlines about suicides, crimes and celebrity relationships. And whether they were true or not no longer mattered.

Fast forward to today and the people whose job it is to capture our attention have had almost 200 years to refine their craft. These are the *attention merchants*.[1] They design apps and adverts with a single purpose in mind: grabbing and holding our attention long enough to feed us adverts. And they've been breathtakingly successful, even when it looked as though everything was working against them. For example, there was a mass *counter-culture* movement in the 1960s, with millions of young people turning their backs on consumerism and corporate greed. What did the corporations do? They sold these young people the idea that to be a true counter-culture kid you had to buy *Pepsi* rather than *Coke*. When the feminist movement started to take off in the 1960s and 70s, they used it to sell women cigarettes. Now, they use fear, greed, humour, envy, sex – anything to control our attention.

But there was always one area of human life that remained free from their grasp. When we talked to friends, family or work colleagues, the attention we gave each other was private. Not anymore. The invention of the *smartphone* means that now even our conversations are monitored and monetized. Our preferences, connections and clicks are used to generate ever more targeted adverts on platforms like Facebook, Instagram, YouTube and Google. As Banksy put it: 'They have re-arranged the world to put themselves in front of you.'[2]

However, these corporations know that there is always a deal at the heart of their business – a deal between us and them. It's based on the very same principles that Benjamin Day used in 1833 – then it was newspapers, now it's apps. The deal is this: They give us apps for free and we give them our attention. We will even tolerate adverts. But the question more and more people are asking is: *Do we really give our attention to our phones or do our phones simply take it?*

Gambling on notifications

It's hard to picture someone less likely to be found rolling dice in a casino than B.F. Skinner. Skinner was a nerdy psychologist from the 1950s who identified the psychology of gambling addiction. He put hungry pigeons in a small box with a disc which would deliver a food pellet when it was pecked. The hungry pigeons would quickly work out that pecking the disc meant food, so they would keep pecking it.

Using this system, Skinner could control exactly how and when the food pellet was delivered. That's how he discovered the addictive nature of something he called *variable ratio reinforcement*.[3] This is when a reward is given at varying intervals determined by a random number of pecks on the disc. So, the pigeon would get a food pellet after 6 pecks, then again after 14 pecks, then after 9 pecks, and so on – with each number of pecks needed for the next reward varying at random. When he did this, he found it was so addictive that the pigeons would continue pecking the disc long after the rewards had stopped being given altogether.

The reason this reward schedule is so addictive is because, just like gambling, you know there's a reward coming at some point. In fact, that reward could always arrive the very next time you put a coin into the slot machine. So, the urge to keep going, just 'one more time', is almost irresistible. One more coin could mean the big pay-out.

Now apply that to your phone. If you keep checking it, at some point you'll be rewarded with a notification that someone has liked your post, or requested to be your friend, or sent you a message. These rewards could always come the very next time you check your phone. That's addictive, just like waiting for a pay-out on a slot machine. It's constantly drawing your attention back to the app. And none of this happened by chance. These notifications were built into the apps exactly because of their addictive qualities. They were designed to keep you hooked and sell you adverts.[4] That's why so many apps are free, because – remember – you're not Instagram's customer, you are the product that they are selling to their advertisers.

Being liked

Believe it or not, there's a good reason for suggesting that the rewards on your app are actually more addictive than the cash rewards from a casino. That's because the rewards on your app – those notifications about *likes*, new followers and new messages – are all about connection with other people. Our need for acceptance and connection with other people is built into our DNA. It's an evolutionary thing – you would not have survived on your own. Acceptance and connection with your community was literally a life or death issue. So, each phone notification is a reward that's working at the deepest human level. It's not true that being left out of your friends' Instagram network is a life or death issue, but it can feel true because it's built into your DNA. So, it's really not surprising that so many of us obsessively check our phones to monitor how accepted and connected we are.

Once your mind is conditioned by these rewards, things move up a level. Now, just the thought of your phone is enough to generate the pleasurable reward feelings. This is called craving.[5] You can check this out yourself by taking your phone out, leaving it on the desk in front of you and staring at it. If you find it difficult to resist picking up the phone, you're feeling the craving that is built on anticipating the rewards you might get from checking your messages and posts. If you find it *impossible* not to pick it up, you've proven something Skinner was convinced of – you no longer have free will. You're no longer deciding where to direct your attention, your phone is. Or, more accurately, it's the people designing the addictive apps who are dictating where you direct your attention.

Facebook is not real life

You might think that, if being connected and accepted by your community is important, then surely the connection you get from social media should work just as well as any real-life, face-to-face social contact. But you'd be wrong. We all know, as we're scrolling through the posts of our friends, that this is not the full story of their life. They are unlikely to post something about how bad their diarrhoea was this morning, or how they woke up in a cold sweat last night, terrified that no one likes them.

Online, we're given a steady stream of the edited highlights of everyone's life. In fact, the highlights of the highlights – the beach holiday without the mosquitoes, the super-selfie on a night out without the loneliness of returning to an empty apartment. Even the person who publishes multiple posts about their day is unlikely to be revealing more than about 10 minutes out of 24 hours.[6]

But the problem is that knowing all this – knowing that we're only seeing the edited highlights – doesn't help us. This is due to our instinctive response to create stories based only on the information immediately in front of us. The Nobel prize-winning behavioural economist Daniel Kahneman calls this *'What You See Is All There Is'*.[7] To show how this works, he asks people the following question about a person called *Mindik*: 'Will Mindik be a good leader? She is intelligent and strong...'

Most people will instinctively answer *yes*. But think about the difference between how easy it was to come to that conclusion and how much you really know about *Mindik*. What if the next two adjectives to describe her are *corrupt* and *cruel*? 'Will Mindik be a good leader? She is intelligent and strong, corrupt and cruel.'

Our mind doesn't feel the need for any more information before coming to a conclusion. Our first response should have been to ask: *What else do I need to know? What exactly should a good leader be like?* But instead our instinct is to create a story just from the information we have right in front of us. And then to jump to a conclusion.

Now apply this idea to the carefully controlled fragments of information that other people post online. You can see how our minds will be busy making up stories about the fabulous life that everyone else is leading. It doesn't matter how often we remind ourselves that there is information missing – our minds are too powerfully attuned to creating stories just from the information right in front of us. Your day will almost never measure up to the best ten minutes of someone else's, so it's not hard to see how trawling through social media can lead to anxiety and depression.

The counter-revolution

There is a growing movement to claim back our attention. One of its leaders is Tristan Harris, a former Google employee who was trained in the *Stanford Persuasive Technology Lab*. When you listen to what he has to say, you realize there's nothing easy about fighting back against corporations like Google and Facebook. You're up against large teams of the best minds in the world, working flat out to create technology that you will be unable to resist. Even more daunting is the fact that, as well as their human intelligence, you're up against the artificial intelligence that comes from the big data they have access to. It's this artificial intelligence that can use your preferences, connections and clicks to predict all kinds of things about you – the way you're going to vote, whether you're about to leave your job, whether you're pregnant, even whether or not you're gay...before you're aware of it yourself.[8]

Once the technology has made these predictions, it chooses which Facebook and Instagram posts you see. It decides which YouTube videos are going to be the most irresistible to you. These are the videos that are recommended to you – to watch next – to keep you hooked. And the problem is that every moment of your attention it captures is a moment you are not paying attention to something else. Something from real life.

This is not about how evil phones are. We all know the huge benefits they bring. This is about making sure that you're using your phone when you want to, not when it wants you to. It's about refusing to give away your attention because of the tricks described above. Your attention is too important to give away thoughtlessly. Google and Facebook know this – they made a combined $1,238 billion from it in 2017.[9] That's the revenue from advertising which they made from us once they had captured our attention.

Becoming an analogue revolutionary

One of the most powerful ways of making sure your phone doesn't take control is to make a conscious decision to have analogue experiences. These are experiences which do not involve digital technology. For example, using an analogue alarm clock means you don't start every day by reaching for your phone, leading to a needless early morning swipe session. Analogue gaming involves going back to board games and experiencing more real-life social interaction. Analogue music might involve listening to a vinyl album – with no skipping or shuffling tracks – so that you begin to understand more fully what your favourite artist is trying to say in their music. There's even analogue reading – that just means picking up a book!

Of course, the ultimate analogue experience is human. You could make a conscious decision to increase your analogue social interactions. And a good way to start is to *stop liking* people's posts. This may seem to you like social suicide, but the evidence suggests you'd be wrong. The problem with *liking* posts is that it feels like social interaction but it isn't. At least, it's not the kind of social interaction which we need in order to feel good.[10] Online social interaction is not the same as real life. It's like drinking sea water to quench your thirst. The more you drink, the more dehydrated you become. The more you rely only on social media for human connection, the lonelier you feel. That's why a recent study of 5,208 Facebook users found that the people who hit the *like* button the most have the worst mental health.[11]

So, *stop liking* people on your phone. Instead, if a friend has posted something awesome, arrange to meet up and tell them how much you like it. Tell them to their face. And, while you're there, spend time with them and give them your attention. Think about that phrase *give them your attention*. It highlights how valuable attention is – it's a gift that you can choose to give someone. So, don't give it away to your phone without thinking. Give it to the analogue experiences that will bring you real satisfaction.

William James was a hugely influential philosopher and one of the pioneers of psychology. He died in 1910, so he didn't have to think too much about the effect of phones, yet his understanding of attention is more relevant than ever. He wrote: 'My experience is what I agree to attend to.'[12] Try replacing the word *experience* with the word *life*. The decision about what you pay attention to is a decision about the kind of life you want to lead. Join the counter-revolution. Join the people all over the world who are claiming back control over their attention – claiming back their lives.

Chapter summary

★ In the 1830s a whole new business model was pioneered, using *clickbait* and *fake news*.

★ Today, phone technology uses notifications, based on our need for *human connection* and *acceptance*, to make phones as addictive as possible.

★ Social interaction on phones is *not the same as real life*. For example, we make up stories about other people's lives based only on the edited highlights of their day.

★ Our *attention* is valuable. Corporations like Facebook and Google use it to sell advertising. And the things you choose to pay attention to dictate what kind of life you lead.

★ *Analogue experiences* are the key to fighting back against the phone technology designed to keep us glued to our phones.

★ The most powerful analogue experience is *human interaction*. When you stop *liking* people's posts, you stop fooling yourself that you're getting the social interaction you need.

Join (or Leave) a Group

A girl decides to take a picture of herself with no clothes on. Then she sends this picture to a boy. She's had lessons at school about the dangers of sexting. She knows there is risk. She suspects that this boy is not completely trustworthy. But she still does it. Why?

The answer to this question has its roots in the trial of Adolf Eich-mann. A Nazi war criminal, he had specialized in organizing the transportation of Jews to death camps.[1] His trial was televised and watched by thousands of Americans, one of whom was a young psychologist called Stanley Milgram. Milgram went on to carry out a set of experiments that are among the most famous in the history of psychology. He found that most people were prepared to administer what they thought to be lethal electric shocks to a stranger when they were told to do so by a researcher in a lab coat. But recent interpretation of the results of these studies suggests that Milgram might have been entirely wrong in the conclusions he drew.

One of the most chilling aspects of watching the Eichmann trial on TV was the way it showed that Eichmann was not a monster, not a seething, hate-filled human – at least not on the surface. Watching him during the trial, it appeared that, in many ways, he was quite ordinary. This was scary because what it suggested is that perhaps any of us, given the right circumstances, could do unspeakably evil things, like him.[2] And this is what Milgram picked up on. It's what he decided to test in his experiments. He was asking the question: *If we're put in the correct conditions, could we all be evil?*[3]

Milgram sat people in front of a shock machine that had switches ranging from 15 volts to 450 volts. They were told that they were taking part in an experiment to test the effect of punishment on memory. There was a stranger in the next room, strapped into a chair and wired up to the shock machine. Milgram told people to give the stranger a shock if they made a mistake on the memory test. The more mistakes the stranger made, the greater the voltage punishment.

These were ordinary people. They had accepted money to take part in this memory research. But they had been lied to – the experiment was not about memory; it was about them. It was about whether they would obey orders to harm an innocent stranger. The electric shocks were not real and the stranger in the other room was working for Milgram, playing pre-recorded responses at each different shock level, such as: 'Let me out of here. My heart's bothering me. Let me out of here! You have no right to keep me here! Let me out!'

What happened took Milgram completely by surprise. Of the people Milgram tested, 65% administered what they thought to be a fatal 450-volt shock to a stranger in another room when told to do so by a university researcher in a white lab coat.

Where Milgram went wrong

But here's where things start to go wrong. Eichmann is quoted as saying: 'It was unthinkable that I would not follow orders.'[4] This theme came up time and again in his trial. This is what Milgram picked up on – the idea that people stop thinking when they're following orders. Milgram used this to explain the results from his experiments, arguing that the people who had flicked the switch when ordered to give a 450-volt shock to a stranger had given up thinking for themselves.[5] He said that, rather than think for themselves, these people handed over all the responsibility for their actions to a university researcher who was giving the orders. As long as they felt that the researcher was in charge, they would switch off their own moral thinking and do anything they were told.

What Milgram was arguing was that we could all do evil things if we were given orders by someone we saw as having legitimate authority over us; because, when we carry out orders from this kind of person, we don't feel personally responsible for our own actions.

This conclusion makes so much sense that it has lasted for over 50 years. But here's why it may be completely wrong. In Milgram's experiment there were four set statements that the researcher used if the participants protested and asked to stop:

1. Please continue.
2. The experiment requires you to continue.
3. It is absolutely essential that you continue.
4. You have no other choice but to continue.

These statements were used in sequence, so that the more the participant protested, the further down the list the researcher would go. But Professor Stephen Reicher makes the simple yet profound observation that only the last of these is actually an order.[6] The first one – 'Please continue' – is a request. Two and three are justifications, pointing out that continuing is part of what's required for the experiment. The last one is the only actual *order*, telling the participant that the only way forward is to continue shocking the stranger.

So, if this is all about the way humans stop thinking and blindly obey authority figures, that last order – 'You have no other choice but to continue' – should have been the most effective at making people continue shocking the stranger. And yet the opposite is true. This order was the only one which had no effect at all. Everyone who was told 'You have no other choice but to continue' refused to obey this command.[7]

Which voice should we listen to?

To explain this, Professor Reicher reframes the Milgram experiments in terms of the voices that the participant is exposed to. On the one hand, there is the voice of the experimenter, impressing on the person in front of them the importance of the research at a prestigious university: *The experiment requires you to continue.* The other voice is that of the stranger being shocked in the other room and pleading to be let out: *Let me out of here. My heart's bothering me. Let me out of here! You have no right to keep me here! Let me out!* When it's put like this, you can see that it's less about whether someone will simply obey an order, and more about which voice they will respond to. Do they listen to the researcher or to the stranger? How do they decide?

To figure out how people decide which voices to listen to, you need to know about *social identities*.[8] Our sense of who we are is made up of our *personal identity* but also a whole series of *social identities*. These spring from all the groups that we're part of. Some of them are formal, like being a football fan. Some are informal, like being part of a particular friendship group. Some may feel as though they are fixed, like being *English* or *Black*. And some might form and dissolve in minutes, like the sudden sense of togetherness that sometimes springs up when people are sitting on a train that's been delayed. It's these social identities which often dictate what we believe and how we act.[9]

Eichmann's choice was between the voices of the German Reich and voices of the Jewish people. The German Reich was central to his social identity, so these were the only voices he chose to hear. His very last words – just before execution – started with: 'Long live Germany, long live Argentina, long live Austria. These are the three countries with which I have been most connected and which I will not forget'.[10] These were his social identities and all his evil actions were built on them.

The people in the Milgram study were interested in taking part in psychological research and they knew they were working together with the researcher on this. During the experiment this shared purpose created a social identity based on carrying out the research. This is important because it means that, when listening to the two voices – the researcher and the stranger – it's the researcher who most of the people listened to. It's also why the statements which pointed out this shared purpose (e.g. *The experiment requires you to continue*) were so powerful.

How the Milgram findings explain sexting

A recent Twitter thread began with a police officer explaining how she had just spent several hours with two girls who had sent nude images of themselves to boys at their school. The boys had promptly sent the pictures to all their friends, and the girls were devastated. The thing is, these girls had attended lessons at school where they were warned about the dangers of sending nude images to other people. They were even vaguely aware that it was illegal both to send the images and for the boys to distribute them. Yet they still did it.

Think about the competing voices that these girls were exposed to. There are the adults (teachers, probably parents too) telling the girls: *Never send nude pictures to boys at school, even if you trust them; it's dangerous and illegal.*

Then there are the people in the girls' friendship group – what were they saying? The police officer on Twitter pointed out that sending nude pictures is often seen as a completely normal part of being in a relationship. So, the voices from the friendship group of these girls would have been saying: *It's no big deal – it's what our group does.*

Finally, there are the boys. The police officer quoted some of the things the boys had said to the girls: *Everyone else sends nude pictures – if you don't do it, we'll tell everyone you're frigid.*

Which voices are most important to the girls? Which voices do they identify with most strongly? Certainly not the teachers. That's why the school had failed in this case. So, we're left with the friendship group and the boys. It hardly mattered which of these voices the girls responded to because they were both saying the same thing. They were both saying that sending nude pictures is normal for their group.

But notice the further threat. What the boys are really saying is: *Sending nudes is what your group does – if you don't do this, we'll let your group know that you're different, and you won't be part of the gang anymore.* Imagine how scary that is – it's threatening their social identity, their sense of who they actually are.

And, let's not forget that the boys themselves are working within another social group. They have their own social identities, which in this case probably involves pressuring girls into sending them pictures. They too risk a lot by rejecting this group identity.

So, most of Milgram's participants gave a 450-volt shock to a stranger. These girls sent nude pictures to boys. They both listened to the voices they identified with and that drove their actions. Before he carried out his study, Milgram asked a group of psychiatrists to predict how people would act in his experimental set-up. The psychiatrists predicted that about 1 person in 1,000 would go all the way up to giving a 450-volt shock to a stranger.[11] As we've seen, they were spectacularly wrong. Similarly, we might think that sending a nude picture to a boy at school is so foolish that only a few stupid, reckless teenagers would do it. We would be spectacularly wrong.

How to make the right decision more often

Obviously, there is no easy way out of the pressure to listen to the voices from the groups that we identify with. The situation those girls were in was difficult to deal with. So, the first thing to say is that any of us who have done things we regret due to the pressure of our group should not beat ourselves up about it – there are powerful forces at work. What we *should* do is figure out some ways of making it less likely that we'll do something we regret in the future.

Firstly, take a look at the groups you are currently part of. Which of them do you feel are the most positive? These should be any groups which are important to you and where you feel you are valued. It might be a large group, or it might be one other person. If you're lucky enough to be part of something positive like this, work at strengthening that group's social identity. This is easily done by being more proactive about looking out for the other people in your group – check whether they need any help, take a bit of time to listen to them, be the one to initiate face-to-face meet-ups.

Secondly, think about any unhealthy groups that you are part of. These will be groups where you are not valued, and where behaviours and ideas that make you feel uncomfortable are seen as normal. If you can, leave the group. But sometimes that's not so easy – it might be a group defined by where you live or what you look like, or a whole host of reasons. However, what you *can* do is try to reduce your dependence on that group. Don't make that group part of who you are, part of your social identity. Don't invest your time and energy in it. See the group for what it is and think of ways to get out of being sucked into behaviours you don't agree with.

When the police officer tweeted about the two girls sending nude pictures, there was a reply from someone called *Mandy J* which the officer and lots of other people liked. Mandy J had asked her niece what food she didn't like. The answer was *celery* – her niece hated celery. So, Mandy J then asked her niece: *If everyone around you was eating celery and telling you you're really missing out, would you start eating celery?* Apparently, the answer to this was pretty straightforward: *No.* Mandy J then said to her niece: *Every time you're in an uncomfortable situation, think of celery.*

So, start with celery. But if celery doesn't work, think about getting some of these techniques ready in advance:

- Join forces with a trusted friend to refuse to go along with something you're uncomfortable with.
- Don't turn up to the party that you know will go wrong.
- Get some phrases ready along the lines of: *You really think I'm going to do that?*
- Confide in a trusted adult when things are getting out of hand.

Most of all, just being aware of the power of groups and social identities is going to help you deal with negative groups.

Thirdly – if you can – join more groups. When you think about it, if your social self is made up of lots of different social identities, it lessens the likelihood that any single social identity is going to have power over you. If your sense of self is made up of not just a single friendship group but also from identifying with your family, a gaming community, an activist group, an online community, a sports or fitness group, an art or drama club, a reading group, etc., then no single group is going to be able to dominate you. Think about what interests you and go with that; find groups that already exist or create new groups.

If all else fails, look for other people who seem to be isolated. When people who find it difficult to fit in come together, they often form the most interesting groups of all.

Chapter summary

★   Some behaviours, such as *sexting*, seem hard to explain.
★   Each group that we feel part of gives us a *social identity*. We all have a strong instinct to listen to the voices of other people in the groups which are important to us.
★   If the people in our groups are telling us that sexting is normal, it becomes very hard to go against them, because that means *questioning our very identity*.
★   We need to question whether the groups we belong to are good – that is, do they give us social identities which make us feel *valued* and help us to be *someone we like*?
★   Being *part of a lot of groups* is useful because it means that we are not dependent on any single group to provide us with a sense of identity.
★   Sometimes it's hard to leave a group which we know is not good. But looking for *allies*, getting *pre-set phrases* ready, and thinking about *celery* can all help.

Ask Someone If They're Okay – Twice

It was her first day at a new school and Natalie Hampton was unsure where she was supposed to be. A boy stopped her in the hallway and asked her if she needed any help finding her class. She says that this small act of kindness saved her life.[1]

What the boy didn't know is that she had left her previous school because she'd been bullied so badly that she had become suicidal. She'd been kicked, punched, threatened, isolated – driven to despair.

There must have been people all around and every opportunity to pass Natalie by. And the boy didn't know how Natalie was going to react. For all he knew, she might have been annoyed that someone thought she needed help. She might have felt threatened that a boy was trying to hit on her. She might have completely blanked him. But, in fact, she was more grateful for his kindness than he will ever know. Natalie is now an anti-bullying activist, app developer, and the CEO of a successful non-profit called *Sit With Us, Inc.*

The thing is, kindness is a wellbeing issue because it's in your genes. Strong social networks, built on kindness, meant that early human communities were more likely to survive through the harsh times.[2] So, being kind has thousands of years of human evolution behind it. And that's why it makes us healthier,[3] less depressed,[4] less stressed,[5] less anxious,[6] less likely to be bullied[7] and even physically stronger.[8]

How to be kind #1: *Set boundaries*

The people who are the most likely to be kind have very clear boundaries. That is, boundaries about what is, and what is not, okay. This is a fact, and for many people it's a shocking one.[9] That's because we tend to think of *rules* and *boundaries* as the kind of things that strict, harsh people use. But it's these boundaries that allow someone to be kind to others without being walked all over. And that's important, because allowing people to walk all over you will cause resentment and pain, which will kill kindness.

For example, imagine a friend of yours is having a hard time with her roommate. She's staying over a lot to get away from the roommate and rant to you about it. You're showing kindness by giving her space in your home and giving her your time as you listen to her troubles. But it's beginning to take its toll on your ability to keep up with your studies. It's also starting to affect your own relationship with your boyfriend or girlfriend. The boundary here is to say, *If you're ever in real trouble, you know you can always come here. But if it's because you need to rant, I'm going to have to ask you to keep that till the weekend when we meet up.* Of course, saying things like this is likely to cause upset, but the alternative is that you become increasingly resentful and maybe lose the friendship altogether. Once the boundaries are set, you will be able to be so much kinder – when you do meet up, you'll be able to listen and offer sympathy with heartfelt sincerity.

When you know that a boundary needs to be set, and a difficult conversation is coming up, one of the best ways to make it happen effectively is to practise.[10] That might mean rehearsing what you need to say in front of a mirror, or role-playing it with a trusted friend. Get the actual phrases ready that you're going to use, and also some follow-up statements that don't let you backslide, such as *I'm sorry you feel that way*.

How to be kind #2: *Start small*

Given how tricky it can be, it's best to start with small acts of kindness.[11] That might mean giving a compliment or a word of encouragement to someone close to you. If you get things going like this, your confidence to perform further acts of kindness is really boosted.[12]

Gradually, you can build up to bigger things, such as starting up a conversation with someone who looks a bit lost or alone, taking the time to listen to a friend, making a phone call to someone you know lives alone, buying a coffee for a work colleague, or organizing an event to cheer someone up. You do need to mix it up, because if you carry out the same act of kindness repeatedly it's likely to feel like something you *have* to do, rather than something you *choose* to do.[13] That means it will lose its sparkle. The trick is to keep looking out for opportunities to be kind. And once you do, the possibilities are pretty much endless.

How to be kind #3: *Make sure it brings you closer*

Because of the evolutionary basis to kindness, it makes sense that we tend to get the most satisfaction when our kindness helps us to get closer to the person we're being kind to.[14] This means that giving someone the money to go and buy a cup of coffee is not going to be as satisfying as taking a friend out and buying their coffee for them while you sit and chat. As you can see, this calls into question the idea of carrying out acts of random kindness. Of course, it's great to be kind in any situation, but we get more of a warm glow of happiness when the act is not so random but is purposefully chosen to bring us closer to someone.

To use another example, this means that it's better to ask a homeless person if they would like something to eat, and then buy them something they'd like, than to simply drop some money into their cup as you walk by. The act of speaking with another person in need and interacting with them in a meaningful way brings us closer to them, even if just for a few minutes, and that's where our own sense of wellbeing comes from.

How to be kind #4: *Ask twice*

When someone says, *How are you?*, do they really want to know? Often, they're just being polite, and we know that the correct answer is something like, *Fine* or, *I'm good*. We get so used to this that we even do it with our friends. That's why asking someone twice is so powerful.

How are you?

I'm fine.

You sure you're okay?

This follow-up is a simple way of telling the other person that you're not just being polite – you really do want to know if they're okay. Often it can allow people close to us to tell us that they're not okay.[15] And that's one of the kindest things you could do for them.

Kindness makes you vulnerable

The thing is, Cinderella is right – it *does* take courage to be kind.[16] That's because being kind is all about connecting with other people. And as soon as you try to connect with others, you become vulnerable – there is a risk of rejection and hurt. Even the smallest moments of rejection can hurt, such as a passing stranger blanking you when you smile at them.[17] In fact, it doesn't even matter if you like the person who's rejecting you – you still feel the pain.[18] And it really does feel painful, because rejection activates the same parts of the brain as physical pain.[19]

Being open to vulnerability means you're the one to start a conversation that might lead to a new friendship. You're the one who is the first to say *I love you*. You're the one who asks someone if they're okay, and then asks if they're *sure* they're okay. But all this also means that you're the one with the deep, meaningful friendships that make life worth living.

As well as requiring courage to be kind, people also need courage to *receive* kindness. These two things – giving and receiving kindness – both require a bit of courage for the same reason: Making human connections is a risky business. Think back to Natalie Hampton and the boy who stopped to ask her if she needed help. Natalie was used to people being hateful towards her, so her initial instinct may well have been suspicion: Was this boy about to make fun of her? Would he expect something in return for his help? Or was he simply being kind? Being open to this last possibility, and accepting kindness, is not always easy. You need to be aware of this and to be open to the possibility of rejection, without getting hurt so badly that you give up trying to be kind.

How to survive and thrive when your kindness is rejected

Firstly, assume that other people – everyone – is doing the best they can. This means that the person who has rejected or just ignored your kindness is struggling with something and doing the best they can. Whether it's true or not, this often helps to make us feel better about the way other people act.[20] The thing is, people who are happy will rarely react to kindness in a negative way. So, even if it feels like the last thing you want to do, try to empathize with the person who has rejected your kindness – try to feel for them.

Secondly, avoid any self-criticism, such as: *Why did I say that? Why was I so stupid? I should've known that wouldn't work.*[21] Instead, if you've been hurt by a rejection of your kindness, try to acknowledge that feeling without allowing it to overwhelm you. And allow it to pass. Because it will pass, and all the more quickly if you don't try to suppress it.[22]

Finally, try to completely reframe any rejection of your kindness and see it as a triumph. Because it's showing you something really important: that you're courageous enough to be vulnerable. All the way back in 1910, US President Theodore Roosevelt made a speech where he spoke about *The Arena*.[23] This is a name for the imaginary *space* you're in when you're daring to be vulnerable, daring to make human connections – daring to be kind.

The Arena is where we're all most likely to get hurt, most likely to be marred by the *dust and sweat and blood* of everyday life. But it's also the place where we're most likely to find joy and love and belonging. The Arena is for people of 'great and generous emotion...

who quell the storm and ride the thunder'.[24] In other words, it's the place where we are most fully alive. And one, sure-fire, way that you know you've been brave enough to get into The Arena is when a kindness you've shown is rejected or ignored. That's why it's a triumph. It means you're strong. In fact, it means you're awesome. So, keep being kind, and keep being vulnerable – it's what makes us fully alive, and it might just save someone's life.

Chapter summary

★   Being kind is *built into our genes*. That's why it makes us healthier, less depressed, less stressed, less anxious, less likely to be bullied and even physically stronger.

★   People who are effective at being kind have clear *boundaries* about what is, and what is not, okay.

★   It's best to start with *small* acts of kindness and build them up slowly.

★   The best acts of kindness are those which bring us *closer* to other people.

★   A very effective act of kindness is to ask those around you if they're okay – *twice*. This is because asking the second time shows them that we are not just being polite – we really do want to know if they're okay.

★   It's possible that our acts of kindness will be met with rejection and even hostility. One way to deal with this is by seeing any such rejection as a mark of our own *courage* – it means we have been brave enough to make ourselves *vulnerable*.

Thank Your Way Out of Chaos

When Donald Trump was speaking at a rally, he told his supporters to knock the crap out of anyone who was getting ready to throw a tomato at him.[1] During the same campaign, Hilary Clinton labelled half of Trump supporters – that's around 30 million Americans – as racist, sexist, homophobic, xenophobic and Islamophobic and said they belong in a basket of deplorables.[2]

In the UK, people who voted to leave the European Union (EU) were accused of being *the lizard-brain of Britain – angry-looking, whey-faced blokes in suits,*[3] who are worse than Nazis.[4] Celebrities lined up to accuse older people of betraying the young,[5,6] with calls to ban old people from voting at all.[7] After the EU referendum, UK Prime Minister Boris Johnson was strongly condemned for using words like *surrender, betrayal* and *traitor* to describe moves in Parliament to block his Brexit plans. One of the main reasons for the anger towards him was that Jo Cox, a Member of Parliament and pro-EU campaigner, had been murdered only three years earlier by a far-right extremist who saw her as someone *betraying* the white race.

All of this is literally *devilish.* The word *devil* means *to throw across*. It's about separating people – making us all feel like there's a chasm between the people we agree with and those we do not. And it's about throwing accusations across that chasm. Republican vs Democrat, Brexit vs Remain, Young vs Old. With this comes a whole new vocabulary – words like *owned, destroyed, red-pilled, cuckolded, gaslighting, dead naming, slut shaming, toxic masculinity, white feminism,* and many more. It's the vocabulary of separation and accusation.

Then, add *no-platforming* into the mix. This is the policy of banning people from speaking at an event because of their views. So many people have been *no-platformed* at UK universities that the *Equality and Human Rights Commission* brought in new guidance for universities to protect free speech.[8] And this is not about the banning of marginal, extremist thinkers. *Germaine Greer* – an iconic, life-long feminist – had thousands of women campaigning to stop her from coming to speak at their university.[9] Why would they do such a thing? The answer is that, in fighting for women, Germaine Greer clashed with the trans community because she argued that men who have sex reassignment surgery are not women.[10]

But *no-platforming* each other just widens that *devilish* chasm. The more ignorant we become about people who are not in our groups, the less we trust them. Distrust leads to fear and, as that fear grows, we need *safe spaces* to keep us safe from others, and *trigger warnings* to help us avoid their ideas. In other words, the less we listen to each other, the more convinced we become that we should never listen to each other again.

In order to justify *no-platforming*, something else has to be thrown into the mix – *competitive victimhood*.[11] This is a competition for the last prize. A competition to prove that our group is the most helpless.[12] It sounds ridiculous, but there are some good reasons for it. For a start, the more convincing a group's victim story is, the more it can demand that other people are shut down

– the more it can justify *no-platforming*. But also, victimhood brings a sense of moral superiority – it's the others who are the bad bullies, so our group must be the good guys.[13] And we all want to feel like the good guys.

This is dangerous. *Competition* means there must be winners and losers. And that means that it's only winning that really matters. Truth no longer matters. Listening no longer matters. Trying to find common ground and ways to live together no longer matters. Winning the war is all that matters – for both sides. And there are wars raging between groups in countless directions.

These are wars of victimhood and they happen because people have learned to be resentful and fearful. Often these resentments and fears are due to unhealed wounds – sometimes very real, raw wounds. But raging against others does not bring healing, it brings chaos. The way out of this chaos is a magic path called *gratitude*. This is about taking time out to be thankful for the good things that are happening in your life, because this will bring peace, even if just for a few moments. And when you're at peace, you can start to heal and you can think clearly. That doesn't mean ignoring injustice – on the contrary, when you're healed and thinking clearly, you will be far better equipped to address injustice.

Gratitude vs resentment

The reason that gratitude works so well is that it breaks down the bedrock of resentment. Resentment makes us feel dissatisfied with life,[14] unconfident,[15] depressed[16] and anxious.[17] But gratitude is the antidote because it focuses your attention on all the good things you have, rather than the things you *don't* have.[18] People who are more grateful are also less *materialistic*. They're less likely to define their own success by the things they have.[19] And when you stop worrying about getting material things, you're much more likely to spend time developing relationships, which really *will* bring happiness and contentment.[20]

But remember, this does not mean that grateful people just sit back and accept whatever happens to them. Grateful people are not passive; instead they're actively connecting with those around them. They have a heightened awareness of the help they receive from others and they want to help people in return. This leads to deep, meaningful friendships.[21] And something about this active interaction with others also means that grateful people are more likely to achieve their life goals than less grateful people.[22]

So – healing, clarity, confidence, happiness, contentment, friendship and achievement – there's every reason to learn how to be more grateful.

How to be more grateful #1: *The five-minute journal*

When you start to look, often you can find all sorts of everyday things to be deeply grateful for: Maybe you can wear the clothes you want to wear without being attacked by religious groups, maybe you can drive a car anywhere you like without being stopped at a roadblock, maybe you can stay in education for as long as it takes to get the qualifications you need, maybe you can take a shower any time you want to, or choose what food to eat, or turn on a tap to get clean water, or speak freely with your friends any time you need to.

Most (if not all) of these things become so routine that we don't remember to be grateful for them. But an effective way to force ourselves to remember to be grateful for ordinary things is to write them down. A recent study asked people to take five minutes to write about five things they were grateful for that day. They did this each day for three weeks. When these people were compared with others who had been asked to write about neutral events, the grateful people were found to be happier and to have slept better.[23] These were people living with *neuromuscular disease*. If they can use gratitude to increase their wellbeing, then so can all of us. And it only takes five minutes a day.

How to be more grateful #2: *Use the bad*

It's easy to fall into the trap of thinking that gratitude is fine but only if you have a life full of good things to be grateful for. The reason this is so wrong is that there are lots of ways you can use *bad* experiences to develop your gratitude. For example, think about the worst moments in your life – the traumas, the disappoint-ments, the bad relationships, the illnesses, the embarrassments. Think about how much you would have given then to be where you are now. And ask yourself: *What good things did the experience draw out of me that surprised me? Can I find ways to be thankful for what happened to me now, even though I was not grateful at the time? How am I now more the person I want to be because of it?*[24]

You can even think about bad things that have not happened to you. If you're stressed or frustrated, you can try thinking about being transported to a war zone, or receiving a call that someone you love has died, or being in constant pain, or feeling the fear of political oppression where you might be arrested at any moment for your beliefs. These things are real and they're happening to countless people around the world right now. If it were happening to you, just imagine how much you would give to get back to where you are right now – how grateful you'd be.[25]

This is why people who have survived life-threatening illnesses and near-death experiences often emerge with a greater sense of thankfulness for their own life. But again, you don't need the near-death experience – taking some time out to reflect on your own death is enough to help most people realize what a gift it is to be alive and to appreciate it more fully.[26]

Getting past *guilt* and *familiarity*

One of the things that can get in the way of gratitude is *guilt*. People who survive traumatic experiences, where others died, can feel *survivor's guilt*. But you could also feel this kind of guilt when thinking about people in war zones, or those experiencing bereavement, or any situation worse than yours. The guilt comes from wondering why you're so much better off than other people without having had to earn your privileged place. Yet another way guilt can obstruct gratitude is when someone much better off than you is helping you out in a way that you can't repay.

The way to get past guilt is to make the most of the opportunities you have. If someone is helping you and you can't repay them in a material way, repay them by the success you make of the opportunities they're giving you.[27] If you're feeling guilty about the people in a war zone, repay them by making the very best of the opportunities you have in a safe country where you can move around freely with access to education, jobs, healthcare, shops, arts, sports, news and free speech.

A second problem is that the more you think about good things in your life, the more familiar and ordinary they become. As that happens, it becomes harder to be grateful for them. So, how can we keep thinking about the good things without letting them lose their power to make us thankful? The answer is, rather than thinking about positive events, think about why a positive event might never have happened and why it was surprising.[28] For example, spending

15–20 minutes writing about how you might never have met your partner gives you a bigger boost in relationship satisfaction than simply thinking about how great your partner is.[29] This is sometimes called the *George Bailey effect* because he is a character from the film *It's a Wonderful Life* who learns to be grateful for his life by being shown what would have happened if he had never existed.

Gratitude connects

There are still things we don't know about gratitude – there's still a bit of mystery around it. For example, when you ask ordinary people what they're grateful for, they often say things like *my health*, or *learning something new today*, or *a clear blue sky on my way to work*.[30] The question is, who are you thanking? And what this points to is that there's a spiritual element to gratitude – it lifts your soul because you're thanking something which you can't see and which seems to be in charge of the really big stuff.[31]

So, it's not surprising that gratitude is at the heart of most religions. For example, one of the most significant elements of Christianity is called the *Eucharist*. That literally means *thanksgiving*. And it's through the Eucharist that Christians believe they form a connection with God and with each other. The thing is, non-religious people who experience intense gratitude also often report feeling a heightened sense of connectedness to others.[32]

Connectedness is the very opposite of the devilish separation and accusation that comes from competitive victimhood. So, here's the choice: Focus on resentment and keep fighting wars of victimhood. Like picking at a scab, it can feel good in the short term, but it will never bring healing. Or, focus on the things you're thankful for in order to find the peace of mind to heal, and to connect with others. Choose to make the most of all the opportunities you have. Choose to thank your way out of chaos.

Chapter summary

★ *Competitive victimhood* is based on resentment and fear, which often stem from unhealed wounds. But raging against others does not bring healing. It brings *chaos*.

★ The way out of chaos is *gratitude* – that's because gratitude undermines resentment by focusing on the good things we have.

★ We can become more grateful by taking about *five minutes a day* to reflect on the good things which have happened to us.

★ *Bad events* can be used to develop gratitude. For example, we can think about how these experiences helped us develop as a person, or we can imagine really bad things that have *not* happened.

★ Two things that can block gratitude are *guilt* and *familiarity*.

★ There's still some mystery surrounding gratitude as it's closely linked to *spirituality*. When people are feeling a deep sense of gratitude, they often have a *heightened sense of connectedness* with others.

Hug Someone Real

There's a large metal bar suspended just behind a toddler's head...

There are two psychologists, one sitting either side of him. One of them places a white rat in front of the toddler and he's happy to reach out and touch it. But, when he does, the other psychologist bangs the metal bar with a hammer. The sound frightens the toddler and he starts to cry. The psychologist keeps on picking up the rat and placing it right in front of the toddler. Each time the toddler reaches out to it, the metal bar is hit and he jumps in fear. Before long, he's afraid of the rat, even without the sound of the metal bar.[1]

For the two psychologists behind this experiment, it was a triumph. They had proved that fear of any object could be artificially created in a human, using a process called *classical conditioning*. These two psychologists were John Watson and Rosalie Rayner, soon to be husband and wife. This is often thought of as one of the most unethical experiments in the history of psychology. But Watson and Rayner were actually carrying out a much crueller experiment on their own children.

John Watson believed that all human behaviour was best explained by *objective, observable, scientific* methods. But when he applied this principle to the nurturing of children, it gave rise to a twisted, callous set of ideas. He published these ideas in a book called *Psychological Care of Infant and Child*. In it he wrote: 'Never hug and kiss your children...remember that mother love is a dangerous instrument. An instrument which may inflict a never-healing wound.'[2]

Watson's basic idea was that treating children like little adults is the best way to train them for the adult world. Just as children could be trained to acquire phobias, so too could they be trained to behave like adults. The quote also shows his profound distrust of affection. He argued that affectionate touch was likely to transmit emotional problems from parent to child. And the fact that this book was a best-seller when it was published in 1928 shows that many thousands of people were buying into his ideas.

Watson applied these ideas to his own children, insisting that they be brought up without ever receiving affectionate touch either from him or from Rosalie, their mother. This is the experiment he carried out, and it took its toll. All of his children attempted to take their own life. One of his sons succeeded. The surviving son directly attributed his brother's suicide to the fact that their father refused to allow affectionate touch in the family.[3]

Touch is about life or death

If John Watson was cruel to humans, Harry Harlow matched him in cruelty to animals. And yet, as offensive as they were, Harlow's animal experiments were a driving force to overturn the disastrous advice from people like Watson. Harlow wanted to test the idea that affectionate touch is important for children's development. He did this by taking newborn baby monkeys and placing them in a cage on their own. At the far end of the cage were two fake *mothers*. These were actually made of wire and wood with something resembling a face at the top. One of these *mothers* provided nothing but food. It was made of wire with a baby's bottle attached to it. The other provided only comfort in the form of cloth that resembled the touch of a real mother.

Without exception, the baby monkeys clung to the *cloth mother*. They would briefly reach over to the *wire mother* only when desperate for food, quickly returning to cling to the *cloth mother* again.[4] The conclusion was clear – touch, rather than food, is the powerful force which draws a mother and child together. Touch is what a child craves. And without it, there are serious consequences.

These consequences were brought into sharp focus in 1989 when the communist dictator of Romania was overthrown and executed. Around 170,000 children were found in orphanages throughout the country. These orphanages had been left so under-staffed that the children had barely experienced human touch. The results of this neglect were devastating – delayed thinking skills, underdeveloped language skills, severe social and emotional problems, psychiatric disorders and physical issues such as stunted growth and immune system problems.[5,6] Lack of human touch was seen as central to all of these problems.

The neuroscience of touch

The thing is, you have a whole range of receptors for all kinds of different touch experience, such as heat, cold, pain, itch, vibration, pressure, texture and sexual contact. The density of these receptors in different parts of your body makes for different experiences. For example, your fingertips have lots of receptors which can pick up tiny shapes and edges, so you use them when you need to feel fine detail.[7] But why is touch so powerful? Why does a connection – from skin to nerve to brain – have such wide-ranging consequences?

First of all, touch is the most highly developed sense at birth.[8] This means that during this hugely important time in your life it's touch which connects you to the people around you. That means it's touch which lets you know if the world is a safe place or not.

But perhaps most important of all, touch always comes with emotion. When you experience touch, two parts of your brain are activated. One of them – the *somatosensory cortex* – processes the facts. It lets you know where you've been touched and what kind of touch it is. The second brain region – the *posterior insular cortex* – adds the emotion. Different kinds of touch create different kinds of emotion.[9] For example, there is a specialized system of nerve fibres called *C-tactiles*, which are specifically designed to pick up slow-moving, gentle touch on your skin. Basically, these nerves are designed to respond to an affectionate caress and to make you feel positive emotion.[10]

But touch is more complicated than a simple response to nerves being activated on your skin. For example, if a stranger gently strokes you on the arm while sitting next to you on a train, it's likely that, rather than a positive emotion, you're going to feel fear or disgust. And if a girl has been in an abusive relationship, where hugs were used as a way of communicating power and control, she may well continue to feel fear and claustrophobia even when a hug is offered from someone she trusts. In other words, as well as being biologically programmed, the emotions we experience in touch are also learned through experience.

Good touch makes us feel safe

What all of us desperately need is *good touch*. And the goodness of touch starts with the relationship you have with the person you're touching. For example, in one study women were put in an fMRI brain scanner, with an electrode attached to their ankle. Once they were inside the scanner, they were shown either a *blue O* or a *red X*. The blue O meant that no shock was coming; but when they saw a red X, they knew there was a 20% chance of receiving an electric shock.

The threat of an electric shock activates a whole host of systems in the brain, controlling fear, anticipation of pain and self-control. So, from your *right dorsolateral prefrontal cortex* to your *hypothalamus,* your brain is working overtime in response to the threat. That's what the scanner picked up when the women were alone and saw a red X.[11] But these women were also tested holding their husband's hand. And this was where the incredible power of touch could be clearly seen. When they were holding the hand of their husband, their brain activity showed that they barely felt threatened by the imminent shock.

These findings revealed something else. Before the experiment in the scanner was carried out, the couples had filled out a questionnaire designed to indicate the quality of the relationship with their partner. What the researchers found was that the women with the strongest relationships showed the lowest threat response in the scanner. In other words, holding the hand of someone you trust reduces your fear in the face of threat.[12] All of the trust and safety of a close relationship is communicated through touch.

Of course, this is not limited to hand holding. Hugs lower blood pressure[13] and significantly decrease your likelihood of viral infection.[14] They even reduce the negative effects of stress for up to a whole day after you've received the hug.[15] Hugs lead to higher oxytocin levels.[16] This is a hormone associated with drawing our attention to personal relationships.[17] So, hugs are a physical reminder that we have people around us who care. And that has a direct effect on our brain and body.

Good touch says things that words can't

Many primates, such as rhesus monkeys, spend at least 20% of their waking hours grooming each other. On the surface this grooming is to get the dirt and parasites out of each other's fur. But what they're often doing is using this touch to say *thank you* for sharing food, or to soothe each other and let each other know that they're trusted and part of the community.[18]

Just like the monkeys, humans use touch to enhance cooperation and group functioning. This was shown most clearly by a study which measured how often NBA basketball players touched each other during an early season game. Using the amount of touch in that single early game, researchers were able to predict the future success of the basketball teams.[19] Each touch, even though it lasted fractions of a second, told the players that they were trusted. That led to much more cooperative behaviour, which, in turn, led to success.

We often use touch as a more powerful way of saying the things we want to get across.[20] Imagine seeing your best friend for the first time in over a year and trying to explain how you feel rather than simply hugging them.

The risks (and benefits) of touching strangers

Not all touch is carried out between trusting, intimate partners. There has to be a moment when you touch someone for the first time. And there are even moments when you may enter the wild, untamed arena of *stranger-touch*. One experiment carried out in France involved an attractive 20-year-old male approaching young women in a nightclub. He would introduce himself by saying,

Hello. My name is Antoine. Do you want to dance? In one scenario he would touch the woman lightly on her forearm, and in the other he didn't touch her at all. The result was that 43% of the women he didn't touch accepted the invitation to dance, but when touch was involved, that figure went up to 65%.[21]

And that result was replicated when young women were approached on the street and asked for their phone number. Of the women who were not touched, 10% provided their phone number. With a light touch on the forearm, that number went up to 19%.[22]

A classic study from the 1980s showed that, when a waitress briefly touched the shoulder of the diner she was collecting the bill from, she received 8–36% more tips than diners who were not touched.[23] But, as with all touch, the context matters a great deal, especially the dynamics of power. The waitress is serving the diners, so the diners are in a position of power here. That makes it less threatening when the waitress touches them.

However, if a diner touched a waitress, that would be far more likely to cause offence. This is because they could so easily be using their power to impose touch on an unwilling person who is in some ways subordinate to them. This is the same as a boss touching one of her employees. The boss would have to be much more careful using touch than two employees of equal rank. Again, this is because the boss could easily be seen as imposing touch on someone they hold power over.

And yet, in certain professional contexts it would be a great loss to stop using touch at all. For example, you can see how important it is in this quote from a patient, talking about the effect of her doctor touching her during a consultation: 'Being touched made me feel…that they understood, but that they really understood, they weren't just going through the motions of saying "I understand".'[24]

It only gets more complicated...

Every time you touch another human being it's a powerful thing. And, like any powerful thing, touch can go seriously wrong. The *#MeToo* movement is all about touch being misused – sometimes on purpose, sometimes by mistake. It's put human touch under the microscope, raising questions about when and where and how we can touch each other.

There are few rules of human touch which apply everywhere. But that doesn't mean there are no rules at all. In fact, the opposite is true – there are very strict rules about human touch. The difficulty is that these rules change depending on who is doing the touching, who is being touched, how they're being touched, and where the touch is happening.

However, even though it's complicated, there are some interesting studies which may help guide us in the use of touch. For example, in one study people from Finland, France, Italy, Russia, and the UK were shown front and back silhouettes of human bodies. Under each silhouette was a word representing someone from their social network, including: *Partner, Friend, Mother, Father, Sister, Brother* and finally *Stranger*. The people were asked to colour the bodily regions where each of these people would be allowed to touch them.

Unsurprisingly, people were generally fine with their partners touching them anywhere on their body. At the other end of the scale, the only place where the touch of a stranger was seen as acceptable was on the hands. There was some acceptance, from far fewer people, of a stranger touching them on the arms or shoulders. With friends, the acceptable touch extended further, to most of the back and the back of the head.[25]

Being touched by a female was, in general, seen as acceptable on more bodily areas than the touch of a male – by both sexes.

And female same-sex touch was seen as acceptable on most of the body. The results did not vary significantly across all five of these countries, suggesting a fairly universal understanding of the acceptability of touch, at least in Europe. There were very slight variations, with people from the UK showing the smallest range of acceptable touch areas, and Finland the largest.

...and even more complicated

On the red carpet of the 2015 Oscars ceremony, John Travolta walked up to Scarlett Johansson, put his arm around her waist and kissed her. The photo of this encounter went viral and Travolta was almost universally slammed for being *creepy*. During the very same Oscars ceremony, whilst on stage, Travolta held Idina Menzel's face and, again, was widely criticized for the way he had touched her.

What these two incidents point to is the fact that the waist and the face are particularly intimate areas. This was backed up by a study which asked participants about nine different types of touch between men and women in the workplace. Touching the face was the area most likely to be seen as sexually harassing as it has a particularly strong emotional impact. Touching the face signals affection, attraction, flirtation and love. Not far behind this was an arm around the waist, which was also very likely to be taken as inappropriate and harassing. Again, an arm around the waist signals high levels of attraction and flirtation. At the other end of the scale, handshaking conveyed the most formality.[26]

But, of course, it's more complicated even than this. You also have to be aware of huge cultural and individual differences in the acceptance of touch. Although we've seen a relatively consistent use of touch across Europe, a glance around the world will throw up far greater differences. A kiss and a hug are often used to greet someone in Italy whereas, in Japan, a formal bow is normal and touch is much more restricted. In terms of individual differences, people who are comfortable with their body image are typically more open to being touched than those who aren't.[27] *And some people just don't like being touched at all.*[28] *So, yes, it's complicated...*

...but don't give up

The temptation could be to withdraw into a world of *virtual touch* – staying behind a screen, texting friends, liking images, meeting in chat rooms, competing against others via a video game. And, for intimacy, the temptation could be to watch, on screen, the most explosively powerful touch of all – sex. Notice what's happening when someone watches porn – there's a clash of intimacy and loneliness. What you're seeing is the most intimate form of human touch, triggering all kinds of intense emotions in your brain. And yet, most people will be watching it alone. Their real-life experience is one of *lack of human connection, lack of human touch.* The gap between what you're seeing and what you're physically experiencing could not be wider. Staying behind a screen may seem safe but it's anything but. Porn use is linked to loneliness[29] and dissatisfaction with life.[30] This is no wonder, when you're watching intimacy whilst cutting yourself off from human touch.

No one is saying that screens are all bad, but it's vital that all of us take every opportunity to come out from behind them and risk the power of real human touch. Good touch. And that starts with trust. So, if you're lucky enough to already have people in your life that you trust, start there. When you shake hands with them, use both hands. When you hug them, mean it. Extend every opportunity for meaningful, trusting, good touch. And, similarly, extend every opportunity for developing trusting relationships.

If you don't yet have people around you that you trust in this way, it's important not to retreat behind a screen for all of your experiences of connection. Put yourself at risk of meeting people face-to-face. Don't watch intimacy on a screen, on your own. Instead use touch, wherever appropriate, to develop trusting relationships.

Social workers often have to use touch in this way. They are in a particularly difficult situation – the people they are dealing with may be frightened of touch due to past experiences of abuse and very difficult relationships. But they may also be in very great need of comforting, supportive touch. The advice social workers are given is to start tentatively with a light, soft touch on the back of the hand or lower arm. Also, to *offer*, rather than impose, touch. For example, you can ask someone if they need a hug.

None of this is fail-safe – it always comes with the risk of offending or being rejected. But there is a bigger risk: that of not experiencing enough human touch. So, in the end, we all have to risk trusting each other. Close the laptop. Put down the phone. Hug someone real.

Chapter summary

★ Touch is important because it's *the most highly developed sense at birth*. That means it lets us know if the world is a safe place or not during this vital developmental period.

★ Touch always comes with emotion. For example, there is a specialized system of nerve fibres called *C-tactiles*, which are specifically designed to pick up slow-moving, gentle touch on your skin.

★ As well as being biologically programmed, the emotions we experience in touch are also *learned* through experience.

★ What all of us desperately need is *good touch*. And the goodness of touch starts with having a trusting relationship with the person you're touching.

★ Good touch, such as hand holding and hugs from a friend, has a range of health benefits because it's a *physical reminder that we have people around us who care.*

★ Because the rules of human touch are complicated, it's sometimes tempting to stay behind a screen and keep *'safe'* with *virtual touch.* This is an especially big problem with porn, because the clash of intimacy and isolation is linked to *loneliness* and *dissatisfaction with life.*

Thank you...

Thanks to my amazing student focus group: Areeb, Aryan, Diva, Jessie, Laura, Lauryn, Lina, Malaika (*class CEO*), Mary Crystal (*ambassador #1*), Nomsa (*Can I listen to music?*), Ovi (*What is your problem?*), Saaleha and Zainab.

Many thanks to all at JKP, especially James Cherry for signing up this book, and Simeon Hance for steering it through to publication. Thanks also to David Griffiths, Simon Oulton and Anna Gaunt for reading some of these chapters and giving me feedback. I'm also grateful to Charles Landry for encouragement, to Sophie Barrowcliff for her feedback and for helping to put me back together when I'd fallen apart, to Kirsty Lowe who encouraged and helped with the very first chapters, and to everyone who prayed for me and this book – especially the Lanherne gang!

Huge thanks to all the families that put us up in England during the summer of 2019, allowing me time to think and write: the Rowe Hines family, the Dossett family, the Barnes family (*Moggsy!*), the Craig Diacopoulos family and especially the Toruń-Shaws, who also lent us their Land Rover. I'm so grateful to you all for opening up your homes to us.

Thanks to my parents for their huge generosity, especially in helping fund my CBT training and for paying for me to sleep in a massage parlour when I was stranded at Nairobi airport. I'm also very grateful to Gillian Carroll for her ongoing support, not least by ensuring we have wifi!

Huge thanks to my big sister Claire – your advice and encouragement made all the difference. Thanks also to my great friend James Frewin – not only do our late-night talks sort out most of the world's problems, but they also led to this book.

Thanks to my beautiful girls, Lottie and Bea, for their encouragement, advice and general awesomeness. And finally, this book was made clearer, and more accurate, by my wife Sara, to whom I am eternally grateful.

About the Author

Aidan Harvey-Craig has degrees in *Applied Psychology* and *The Psychology of Education*. He has worked as an assistant psychologist in a maximum security prison, as an editor for a global producer of travel information, as a founder of an online business for musicians, as a teacher of Psychology in secondary schools across England and in Africa, as a student counsellor using CBT and solution-focused practice, and as a sandwich stuffer in a café at the Tower of London. He has presented at the *Division of Forensic Psychology Annual Conference* and at the conference of the *Association of Teachers of Psychology*. Aidan has also appeared on the BBC as a finalist on *The UK's Best Part-Time Band,* resulting in the release of the album *Sisyphus*. He has written for the *Legal and Criminological Psychology* journal, *ResearchEd* magazine and the mighty *Stroud News and Journal,* and he blogs at *wellbeinghacks.org*. Currently, he lives and works in Malawi.

Notes

Introduction

1 Ryff, C.D. (2014) 'Psychological well-being revisited: Advances in science and practice.' *Psychotherapy and Psychosomatics 81*(1), 10–28.

2 Braungart, J.M., Plomin, R., Defries, J.C. & Fulker, D.W. (1992) 'Genetic influence on tester-rated infant temperament as assessed by Bayley's Infant Behavior Record: Nonadoptive and adoptive siblings and twins.' *Developmental Psychology 28*(1), 40–47.

3 Schkade, D.A. & Kahneman, D. (1998) 'Does living in California make people happy? A focusing illusion in judgments of life satisfaction.' *Psychological Science 9*(1), 340–346.

4 Lyubomirsky, S., Sheldon, K.M. & Schkade, D. (2005) 'Pursuing happiness: The architecture of sustainable change.' *Review of General Psychology 9*(2), 111–131.

5 Sheldon, K.M. & Lyubomirsky, S. (2019) 'Revisiting the Sustainable Happiness Model and Pie Chart: Can Happiness Be Successfully Pursued?' *The Journal of Positive Psychology.* DOI: 10.1080/17439760.2019.1689421

6 See note 4.

7 See note 4.

8 See note 4.

Wellbeing Hack 1: Name Your Emotions

1 Smith, T.W. (2015) *The Book of Human Emotions: An Encyclopedia of Feeling from Anger to Wanderlust.* London: Profile Books.

2 Gerhardt, S. (2004) *Why Love Matters.* Hove: Routledge.

3 Kashdan, T., Feldman Barrett, L. & McKnight, P. (2015) 'Unpacking emotion differentiation: Transforming unpleasant experience by perceiving distinctions in negativity.' *Current Directions in Psychological Science 24*(1), 10–16.

4 Fan, R., Varol, O., Varamesh, A., Barron, A. *et al.* (2019) 'The minute-scale dynamics of online emotions reveal the effects of affect labeling.' *Nature Human Behaviour 3*(1), 92–100.

5 See note 3.

6 Quoidbach, J., Gruber, J., Mikolajczak, M., Kogan, A., Kotsou, I. & Norton, M.I. (2014) 'Emodiversity and the emotional ecosystem.' *Journal of Experimental Psychology 143*(6), 2066.

7 See note 6.

8 See note 6.

9 Kircanski, K., Lieberman, M. & Craske, M. (2012) 'Feelings into words: Contributions of language to Exposure Therapy.' *Psychological Science 23*(10), 1086–1091.

10 Quoidbach, J., Mikolajczak, M. & Gross, J.J. (2015) 'Positive interventions: An emotion regulation perspective.' *Psychological Bulletin 141*(3), 655–693.

11 Yik, M., Russell, J.A. & Steiger, J.H. (2011) 'A 12-point circumplex structure of core affect.' *Emotion 11*(4), 705–731.

12 RULER (supported by the Yale Center for Emotional Intelligence). *How RULER Works.* Available at http://ei.yale.edu/ruler/how-ruler-works, accessed July 10, 2019.

13 RULER. *RULER Online Platform.* Available at www.rulerapproach.org/solutions, accessed July 10, 2019.

14 Fu, C.-S. (2012) 'What are emotions in Chinese Confucianism?' *Linguistics, Culture and Education 1*, 78—93.

15 Darwin, C. (1872) *The Expression of the Emotions in Man and Animals.* London: John Murray.

16 Ekman, P. (2016) 'What scientists who study emotion agree about.' *Perspectives on Psychological Science 11*, 31–34.

17 Du, S. & Martinez, A. (2015) 'Compound facial expressions of emotion: From basic research to clinical applications.' *Dialogues in Clinical Neuroscience 17*(4), 443–455.

18 See note 17.

19 Ekman, P., Dalgleish, T. & Power, M. (1999) *Basic Emotions: Handbook of Cognition and Emotion.* London: John Wiley and Sons.

20 Burton, N. (2015) *Heaven and Hell: The Psychology of Emotions.* Oxford: Acheron Press.

21 DeBotton, A. *On Love | Digital Season.* Available at www.youtube.com/watch?v=Ctz6e J3Pr94, accessed April 21, 2020.

22 See note 20.

23 Proust, M. (1999) *Time Regained: In Search of Lost Time* (Vol VI Modern Library). London: Random House.

Wellbeing Hack 2: Eat Something You're Looking At

1   Jamil, J. (May 15, 2018). *Twitter.* Available at https://twitter.com/jameelajamil/status/996603187623641090?lang=en, accessed January 18, 2020.

2   Blackmon, M. (2018) 'Jameela Jamil opened up about her struggle with an eating disorder as a teen.' *BuzzFeedNews.* Available at www.buzzfeednews.com/article/michaelblackmon/jameela-jamil, accessed January 20, 2020.

3   Davies, T. & Beeharee, A. (2012) 'The case of the missed icon: Change blindness on mobile devices.' *Proceedings of the SIGCHI Conference on Human Factors in Computing Systems.* DOI: 10.1145/2207676.2208606

4   Neal, D., Wood, W. & Quinn, J. (2006) 'Habits—A repeat performance.' *Current Directions in Psychological Science 15*(4), 198–202.

5   Baker, C. (2018) *Obesity Statistics.* London: House of Commons Library.

6   Centers for Disease Control and Prevention (2018) *Adult Obesity Facts.* Available at www.cdc.gov/obesity/data/adult.html, accessed January 20, 2020.

7   Anorexia & Bulimia Care (2019) *Statistics.* Available at www.anorexiabulimiacare.org.uk/about/statistics, accessed January 20, 2020.

8   Shapiro, S.L., Carlson, L.E., Astin, J.A. & Freedman, B. (2006) 'Mechanisms of mindfulness.' *Journal of Clinical Psychology 62*(3), 373–386.

9   Dunn, C., Haubenreiser, M., Johnson, M., Nordby, K. *et al.* (2018) 'Mindfulness approaches and weight loss, weight maintenance, and weight regain.' *Current Obesity Reports 7*(1) 37–49.

10 Hanson, P., Shuttlewood, E., Halder, L., Shah, N. *et al.* (2019) 'Application of mindfulness in a tier 3 obesity service improves eating behavior and facilitates successful weight loss.' *Journal of Clinical Endocrinology and Metabolism 104*(3), 793–800.

11 Bacon, L. & Aphramor, L. (2011) 'Weight science: Evaluating the evidence for a paradigm shift.' *Nutrition Journal 10*(9). DOI: 10.1186/1475-2891-10-9

12 Orbach, S. (2002) *On Eating*. London: Penguin.

13 Moss, M. (2013) 'The extraordinary science of addictive junk food.' *New York Times.* Available at www.nytimes.com/2013/02/24/magazine/the-extraordinary-science-of-junk-food.html, accessed January 20, 2020.

14 See note 12.

15 Lu, S. (2019) 'The mental snag that makes it seem like food is everywhere, especially if you're overweight.' *The British Psychological Society Research Digest.* Available at https://digest.bps.org.uk/2019/01/07/the-mental-snag-that-makes-it-seem-like-food-is-everywhere-especially-if-youre-overweight/#more-35890, accessed January 20, 2020.

16 See note 12.

17 Annesi, J. & Mareno, N. (2015) 'Improvement in emotional eating associated with an enhanced body image in obese women: Mediation by weight-management treatments' effects on self-efficacy to resist emotional cues to eating.' *Journal of Advanced Nursing 71*(12), 2923–2935.

18 Frayn, M., Livshits, S. & Knäuper, B. (2018) 'Emotional eating and weight regulation: A qualitative study of compensatory behaviors and concerns.' *Journal of Eating Disorders 6*(23). DOI: 10.1186/s40337-018-0210-6

19 See note 12.

20 Robinson, T.N. & Matheson, D.M. (2015) 'Environmental strategies for portion control in children.' *Appetite 88*, 33–38.

21 See note 12.

22 Dugas, J. (2017) *Mindful eating checklist: How to master mindful eating.* International Food Information Council. Available at https://foodinsight.org/mindful-eating-checklist-how-to-master-mindful-eating, accessed January 20, 2020.

23 Rolls, E. (2006) 'Brain mechanisms underlying flavour and appetite.' *Philosophical Transactions of the Royal Society of London 361*(1471), 1123–1136.

24 Aldenderfer, M., Craig, N.M., Speakman, R.J. & Popelka-Filcoff, R. (2008) 'Four-thousand-year-old gold artifacts from the Lake Titicaca basin, southern Peru.' *PNAS 105*(13), 5002–5005.

25 Rumolda, C. & Aldenderfer, M. (2016) 'Late archaic–early formative period micro-botanical evidence for potato at Jiskairumoko in the Titicaca Basin of southern Peru.' *PNAS 113*(48), 13672–13677.

26 History Ireland (n.d.) *The introduction of the potato into Ireland.* Available at www.historyireland.com/early-modern-history-1500-1700/the-introduction-of-the-potato-into-ireland, accessed January 20, 2020.

27 The Little Potato Company (2018) *Origin of potatoes.* Available at www.littlepotatoes.com/blog/origin-of-potatoes, accessed January 20, 2020.

28 Chips, Crums and Specks of Saratoga County History (n.d.) *The story of Saratoga chips and their mythical makers.* Available at http://chipscrumsandspecksofsaratogacountyhistory.com/2013/06/29/saratoga-potato-chip-stories-traditions-myths-and-legends/#fn15-87, accessed January 20, 2020.

29 Saltwork Consultants (n.d.) *Salt and civilisation.* Available at www.saltworkconsultants.com/salt-and-civilisation.html, accessed January 20, 2020.

30 *Time* magazine (1982) *A brief history of salt.* Available at http://content.time.com/time/magazine/article/0,9171,925341,00.html, accessed January 20, 2020.

31 See note 29.
32 See note 30.
33 See note 30.

Wellbeing Hack 3: Watch Your Thoughts

1 Adams, K. (2014) 'Blind ambition.' *BBC Kent*. Available at www.bbc.co.uk/kent/content/articles/2007/08/15/kevin_alderton_feature.shtml, accessed January 20, 2020.
2 Phillips, M. (2013) '200mph blind biker.' *The Sun*. Available at www.thesun.co.uk/archives/news/949064/200mph-blind-biker, accessed January 20, 2020.
3 See note 1.
4 Gornall, S. (2017) 'Skiing by braille.' *Ski* magazine. Available at www.skimag.com/adventure/skiing-by-braille-0, accessed January 20, 2020.
5 Kennerley, H., Kirk, J. & Westbrook, D. (2017) *An Introduction to Cognitive Behaviour Therapy: Skills and Applications*. London: Sage.
6 Beck, J.S. (2011) *Cognitive Behavior Therapy: Basics and Beyond*. New York, NY: The Guilford Press.
7 See note 6.
8 See note 5.
9 Robert, E. (2016) 'The prince of reason.' *Psychology Today*. Available at www.psychologytoday.com/intl/articles/200101/the-prince-reason.
10 Cowan Hill, J. (2018) *How to help tinnitus – 15 tips*. Available at www.youtube.com/watch?v=pVbTfcbWuyQ, accessed January 20, 2020.

Wellbeing Hack 4: Write Yourself a Lifeline

1 Bauman, Z. (2006) *Liquid Times: Living in an Age of Uncertainty*. Cambridge: Polity Press.
2 James, S.L. (2013) 'Bauman's "sensation gatherers" and the significance of work today.' *Reflections, Intersections and Aspirations: 50 years of Australian Sociology*. Paper presented at the TASA Annual Conference Conference.
3 McAdams, D. (2001) 'The psychology of life stories.' *Review of General Psychology 5*(2), 100–122.
4 Erikson, E.H. (1968) *Identity, Youth, and Crisis*. New York, NY: Norton.
5 Waters, T.E.A. & Fivush, R. (2015) 'Relations between narrative coherence, identity, and psychological well-being in emerging adulthood.' *Journal of Personality 83*(4), 441–451.
6 McAdams, D. (2017) *The self as a story*. Available at www.youtube.com/watch?v=yS-DUoyL3KHg, accessed January 20, 2020.
7 See note 6.
8 Habermas, T. & Bluck, S. (2000) 'Getting a life: The emergence of the life story in adolescence.' *Psychological Bulletin 126*(5), 748–769.
9 Habermas, T. & Paha, C. (2001) 'The development of coherence in adolescents' life narratives.' *Narrative Inquiry 11*(1), 35–54.
10 Adler, J.M. (2012) 'Living into the story: Agency and coherence in a longitudinal study of narrative identity development and mental health over the course of psychotherapy.' *Journal of Personality and Social Psychology 102*(2), 367–389.
11 Chandler, M.J., Boyes, M., Ball, L. & Hala, S. (1987) 'The Conservation of Selfhood: A Developmental Analysis of Children's Changing Conceptions of Self-Continuity.' In T. Honess & K. Yardley (eds) *Self and Identity: Perspectives across the Life-Span*. London: Routledge.

12 Kitchener, K.S. & Fischer, K. (1990) 'A Skill Approach to the Development of Reflective Thinking.' In D. Kuhn (ed.) *Developmental Perspectives on Teaching and Learning Thinking Skills.* New York, NY: Karger.

13 See note 10.

14 See note 5.

15 Pennebaker, J.W. & Beall, S.K. (1986) 'Confronting a traumatic event: Toward an understanding of inhibition and disease.' *Journal of Abnormal Psychology 95*(3), 274–281.

16 McKenna, M.H. (1997) 'Symptom as storyteller: Migraine headache and journal writing.' *Dissertation Abstracts International 59*(6-B), 3112.

17 Bodor, N.Z. (2002) 'The health effects of emotional disclosure for individuals with Type 1 diabetes.' Unpublished doctoral dissertation. Austin, TX: University of Texas.

18 Kelley, J.E., Lumley, M.A. & Leisen, J.C.C. (1997) 'Health effects of emotional disclosure in rheumatoid arthritis patients.' *Health Psychology 16*(4), 331–340.

19 Pennebaker, J.W., Kiecolt-Glaser, J.K. & Glaser, R. (1988) 'Disclosure of traumas and immune function: Health implications for psychotherapy.' *Journal of Consulting and Clinical Psychology 56*(2), 239–245.

20 Walker, B.L., Nail, L.M. & Croyle, R.T. (1999) 'Does emotional expression make a difference in reactions to breast cancer?' *Oncology Nursing Forum 26*(6), 1025–1032.

21 Smyth, J.M. (1998) 'Written emotional expression: Effect sizes, outcome types, and moderating variables.' *Journal of Consulting and Clinical Psychology 66*(1), 174–184.

22 Earnhardt, J.L., Martz, D.M., Ballard, M.E. & Curtin, L. (2002) 'A writing intervention for negative body image: Pennebaker fails to surpass the placebo.' *Journal of College Student Psychotherapy 17*(1), 19–35.

23 Kovac, S.H. & Range, L.M. (2002) 'Does writing about suicidal thoughts and feelings reduce them?' *Suicide and Life-Threatening Behavior 32*(4), 428–440.

24 Stroebe, M., Stroebe, W., Schut, H., Zech, E. & van den Bout, J. (2002) 'Does disclosure of emotions facilitate recovery from bereavement? Evidence from two prospective studies.' *Journal of Consulting and Clinical Psychology 70*(1), 169–178.

25 Pennebaker, J.W. (1993) 'Putting stress into words: Health, linguistic, and therapeutic implications.' *Behaviour Research and Therapy 31*(6), 539–548.

26 King, L.A. (2001) 'The health benefits of writing about life goals.' *Personality and Social Psychology Bulletin 27*, 798–807.

27 Boehm, J.K., Lyubomirsky, S. & Sheldon, K.M. (2011) 'A longitudinal experimental study comparing the effectiveness of happiness-enhancing strategies in Anglo Americans and Asian Americans.' *Cognition and Emotion 25*(7), 1152–1167.

28 See note 27.

29 See note 26.

30 Peters, M.L., Flink, I.K., Boersma, K. & Linton, S.J. (2010) 'Manipulating optimism: Can imagining a best possible self be used to increase positive future expectancies?' *The Journal of Positive Psychology 5*(3), 204–211.

31 Lyubomirsky, S., Dickerhoof, R., Boehm, J.K. & Sheldon, K.M. (2011) 'Becoming happier takes both a will and a proper way: An experimental longitudinal intervention to boost well-being.' *Emotion 11*(2), 391–402.

32 Layous, K., Nelson, S.K. & Lyubo mirsky, S. (2012) 'What is the optimal way to deliver a positive activity intervention? The case of writing about one's best possible selves.' *Journal of Happiness Studies 14*(2), 635–654.

33 See note 32.

34 See note 31.

35 McAdams, D.P., Reynolds, J., Lewis, M., Allison, H., Patten, P. & Bowman, J. (2001) 'When bad things turn good and good things turn bad: Sequences of redemption and contamination in life narrative and their relation to psychosocial adaptation in midlife adults and in students.' *Personality and Social Psychology Bulletin 27*(4), 474–485.

36 See note 6.

37 See note 35.

38 See note 35.

39 See note 35.

40 Affleck, G. & Tennen, H. (1996) 'Construing benefits from adversity: Adaptational significance and dispositional underpinnings.' *Journal of Personality 64*(4), 899–922.

41 See note 35.

Wellbeing Hack 5: Use Music on Purpose

1 Seibert, E. (2016) *Why I want to change the world with music therapy*. Available at www.youtube.com/watch?v=47-90fPyQa8&app=desktop, accessed January 20, 2020.

2 See note 1.

3 McFerran, K.S. & Saarikallio, S. (2014) 'Depending on music to feel better: Being conscious of responsibility when appropriating the power of music.' *The Arts in Psychotherapy 41*(1), 89–97.

4 See note 3.

5 McFerran, K. (2019) 'Crystallizing the Relationship between Adolescents, Music and Emotions.' In K. McFerran, P. Derrington & S. Saarikallio (eds) *Handbook of Music, Adolescents, and Wellbeing*. Oxford: Oxford University Press.

6 McFerran, K. (2016) 'Contextualising the relationship between music, emotions and the well-being of young people: A critical interpretive synthesis.' *Musicae Scientiae 20*(1), 103–121.

7 Garrido, S., Eerola, T. & McFerran, K. (2017) 'Group rumination: Social interactions around music in people with depression.' *Frontiers in Psychology 8*, 490.

8 Small, C. (1998) *Musicking: The Meanings of Performing and Listening*. Hanover, CT: Wesleyan University Press.

9 See note 5.

10 Baltazar, M. (2019) 'Musical Affect Regulation in Adolescents: A Conceptual Model.' In K. McFerran, P. Derrington & S. Saarikalio (eds) *Handbook of Music, Adolescents, and Wellbeing*. Oxford: Oxford University Press.

11 Saarikallio, S. & Erkkilä, J. (2007) 'The role of music in adolescents' mood regulation.' *Psychology of Music 35*(1), 88–109.

12 See note 11.

13 See note 11.

14 See note 11.

15 Van den Tol, A.J.M., Edwards, J. & Heflick, N.A. (2016) 'Sad music as a means for acceptance-based coping.' *Musicae Scientiae 20*(1), 68–83.

16 See note 11.

17 See note 11.

18 Lamont, A. (2011) 'University students' strong experiences of music: Pleasure, engagement, and meaning.' *Musicae Scientiae 15*(2), 229–249.

19 See note 11.

20 See note 11.

21 DeNora, T. (1999) 'Music as a technology of the self.' *Poetics 27*(1), 31–56.

22 Saarikallio, S. (2019) 'Music as a Resource for Agency and Empowerment in Identity Construction.' In K. McFerran, P. Derrington & S. Saarikallio (eds) *Handbook of Music, Adolescents, and Wellbeing*. Oxford: Oxford University Press.

23 Bennett, A. & Nikulinsky, L. (2019) 'Wellbeing, Young People, and Music Scenes.' In

K. McFerran, P. Derrington & S. Saarikallio (eds) *Handbook of Music, Adolescents, and Wellbeing*. Oxford: Oxford University Press.

24 Boer, D., Fischer, R. & Strack, M. (2001) 'How shared preferences in music create bonds between people: Values as the missing link.' *Personality and Social Psychology Bulletin 37*(9), 1159–1171.

25 Snell, D. & Hodgetts, D. (2007) 'Heavy Metal, identity and the social negotiation of a community of practice.' *Journal of Community and Applied Social Psychology 17*(6). DOI: 10.1002/casp.943

26 Csikszentmihalyi, M. (2002) *Flow: The Classic Work on How to Achieve Happiness*. London: Rider.

27 Baltazar, M. & Saarikallio, S. (2017) 'Strategies and mechanisms in musical affect self-regulation: A new model.' *Musicae Scientiae*. DOI: 10.1177/1029864917715061

28 Reschke-Hernandez, A.E. (2014) 'Paula Lind Ayers: "Song-physician" for troops with shell shock during World War I.' *Journal of Music Therapy 51*(3), 276–291.

29 DeNora, T. (2019) '"Forever piping songs forever new": The Musical Teenager and Musical Inner Teenager across the Life Course.' In K. McFerran, P. Derrington & S. Saarikallio (eds) *Handbook of Music, Adolescents, and Wellbeing*. Oxford: Oxford University Press.

Wellbeing Hack 6: Stop Dating People Like Your Parents

1 Freud, S. (1938) *An Outline of Psycho-Analysis*. Available at www.icpla.edu, https://icpla.edu/wp-content/uploads/2012/10/Freud-S.-An-Outline-of-Psychoanalysis-Int.-JPA.pdf, accessed February 4, 2020.

2 Sulloway, F. (1983) *Freud, Biologist of the Mind: Beyond the Psychoanalytic Legend*. New York, NY: Basic Books,.

3 Bereczkei, T. & Gyuris, P. (2009) 'Oedipus complex, mate choice, imprinting: An evolutionary reconsideration of a Freudian concept based on empirical studies.' *The Mankind Quarterly 50*(1), 71–94.

4 Eastwick, P., Luchies, L.B., Finkel, E.J. & Hunt, L.L. (2013) 'The predictive validity of ideal partner preferences: A review and meta-analysis.' *Psychological Bulletin 140*(3), 623–665.

5 Shepher, J. (1983) *Incest: A Biosocial View*. New York, NY: Academic Press.

6 See note 5.

7 Keller, L.F. & Waller, D.M. (2002) 'Inbreeding effects in wild populations.' *Trends in Ecological Evolution 17*(5), 230–241.

8 Robinson, M., Kleinman, A., Graff, M., Vinkhuyzen, D.C. *et al.* (2017) 'Genetic evidence of assortative mating in humans.' *Nature Human Behaviour 1*, article 16.

9 See note 3.

10 Bereczkei, T., Gyuris, P. & Weisfeld, G. (2004) 'Sexual imprinting in human mate choice.' *Proceedings of the Royal Society 271*(1544), 1129–1134.

11 See note 10.

12 Wilson, G. & Barrett, P. (1987) 'Parental characteristics and partner choice: Some evidence for Oedipal imprinting.' *Journal of Biosocial Science 19*(2), 157–171.

13 Hepper, E. & Carnelley, K. (2012) 'Attachment and Romantic Relationships: The Roles of Working Models of Self and Other.' In M. Paludi (ed.) *The Psychology of Love*. Santa Barbara, CA: Praeger.

14 Impett, E.A. & Peplau, L.A. (2002) 'Why some women consent to unwanted sex with a dating partner: Insights from attachment theory.' *Psychology of Women Quarterly 26*(4), 360–370.

15 Morgan, H. & Shaver, P. (1999) 'Attachment Processes and Commitment to Romantic

Relationships.' In J.M. Adam & W.H. Jones (eds) *Handbook of Interpersonal Commitment and Relationship Stability*. New York, NY: Plenum.

16 Pietromonaco, P., Greenwood, D. & Feldman Barrett, L. (2004) 'Conflict in Adult Close Relationships: An Attachment Perspective.' In W.S. Rholes & J.A. Simpson (eds) *Adult Attachment: New Directions and Emerging Issues*. New York, NY: Guilford Press.

17 Bowlby, J. (1973) *Attachment and Loss Volume 2. Separation: Anxiety and Anger*. New York, NY: Basic Books.

18 Feeney, J. (1999) 'Issues of closeness and distance in dating relationships: Effects of sex and attachment style.' *Journal of Social and Personal Relationships 16*(5), 571–590.

19 See note 13.

20 Shaver, P.R. & Mikulincer, M. (2012) 'An Attachment Perspective on Morality: Strengthening Authentic Forms of Moral Decision-Making.' In M. Mikulincer & P.R. Shaver *The Social Psychology of Morality: Exploring the Causes of Good and Evil*. Washington DC: American Psychological Association.

21 See note 13.

22 Strauss, A. (1946) 'The influence of parent-images upon marital choice.' *American Sociological Review 11*(5), 554–559.

23 Office For National Statistics (2017) *People who were abused as children are more likely to be abused as an adult*. Available at www.ons.gov.uk/peoplepopulationandcommunity/crimeandjustice/articles/peoplewhowereabusedaschildrenaremorelikelytobeabused asanadult/2017-09-27, accessed January 21, 2020,

24 See note 23.

25 Canning, M. (2007) *Lust, Anger, Love: Understanding Sexual Addiction and the Road to Healthy Intimacy*. Naperville, IL: Sourcebooks.

26 Love, P. & Shulkin, S. (2001) 'Imago theory and the psychology of attraction.' *The Family Journal 9*(3), 246–249.

Wellbeing Hack 7: Paint Your Broken Edges Gold

1 Antony, M. (2011) *When perfect isn't good enough*. Available at www.youtube.com/watch?v=TTbnBmwKuCI, accessed January 21, 2020.

2 See note 1.

3 Flett, G.L. & Hewitt, P.L. (2002) 'Perfectionism and Maladjustment: An Overview of Theoretical, Definitional, and Treatment Issues.' In G.L. Flett & P.L. Hewitt (eds) *Perfectionism: Theory, Research and Treatment*. Washington DC: American Psychological Association.

4 Nepon, T., Flett, G.L. & Hewitt, P.L. (2016) 'Self-image goals in trait perfectionism and perfectionistic self-presentation: Toward a broader understanding of the drives and motives of perfectionists.' *Self and Identity 15*(6), 683–706.

5 Harrington, J. (2016) *Perceptions of perfection*. Available at www.youtube.com/watch?v=huOxk-UhOzo, accessed January 21, 2020.

6 See note 1.

7 Kari, P. (2018) *More than 200,000 teens had plastic surgery last year, and social media had a lot to do with it*. Available at www.marketwatch.com/story/should-you-let-your-teenager-get-plastic-surgery-2018-08-29, accessed January 21, 2020.

8 Sherry, S. & Smith, M.M. (2019) *Young people drowning in a rising tide of perfectionism*. Available at http://theconversation.com/young-people-drowning-in-a-rising-tide-of-perfectionism-110343, accessed January 21, 2020.

9 Curran, T. & Hill, A.P. (2019) 'Perfectionism is increasing over time: A meta-analysis of birth cohort differences from 1989 to 2016.' *Psychological Bulletin 145*(4), 410–429.

10 See note 5.

11 Lessin, D.S. & Pardo, N.T. (2017) 'The impact of perfectionism on anxiety and depression.' *Journal of Psychology and Cognition* 2(1). DOI: 10.35841/psychology-cognition.2.1.78-82

12 Lloyd, S., Yiend, J., Schmidt, U. & Tchanturia, K. (2014) 'Perfectionism in anorexia nervosa: Novel performance based evidence.' *PLoS One* 9(10), e111697.

13 See note 11.

14 Fry, P.S. & Debats, D.L. (2009) 'Perfectionism and the five-factor personality traits as predictors of mortality in older adults.' *Journal of Health Psychology* 14(4), 513–524.

15 Hill, A.P., Hall, H., Duda, J. & Appleton, P.R. (2011) 'The cognitive, affective and behavioural responses of self-oriented perfectionists following successive failure on a muscular endurance task.' *International Journal of Sport and Exercise Psychology* 9(2), 189–207.

16 Beevers, C.G. & Miller, I.W. (2004) 'Perfectionism, cognitive bias, and hopelessness as prospective predictors of suicidal ideation.' *Suicide and Life-Threatening Behaviour* 34(2), 126–137.

17 Hewitt, P.L. & Flett, G.L. (1991) 'Perfectionism in the self and social contexts: Conceptualization, assessment, and association with psychopathology.' *Journal of Personality and Social Psychology* 60(3), 456–470.

18 Haring, M., Hewitt, P.L. & Flett, G.L. (2003) 'Perfectionism, coping, and quality of intimate relationships.' *Journal of Marriage and Family* 65(1), 143–158.

19 Hewitt, P.L., Flett, G.L., Sherry, S.B., Habke, M. *et al.* (2003) 'The interpersonal expression of perfection: Perfectionistic self-presentation and psychological distress.' *Journal of Personality and Social Psychology* 84(6), 1303–1325.

20 Derlega, V.J., Metts, S., Petronio, S. & Margulis, S.T. (1993) *Self-Disclosure*. Thousand Oaks, CA: Sage.

21 Anxiety Canada (n.d.) *How to overcome perfectionism*. Available at www.anxietycanada.com/sites/default/files/Perfectionism.pdf., accessed January 21, 2020.

22 Shikatani, B., Antony, M.M., Cassin, S.E. & Kuo, J.R. (2015) 'Examining the role of perfectionism and intolerance of uncertainty in postevent processing in social anxiety disorder.' *Journal of Psychopathology and Behavioral Assessment* 38(2), 297–306.

23 Tetlock, P.E. (2006) *Expert Political Judgment: How Good Is It? How Can We Know?* Princeton, NJ: Princeton University Press.

24 Kwan, P.Y. (n.d.) *Exploring Japanese art and aesthetic*. Available at www.designedasia.com/2012/Full_Papers/Exploring%20Japanese%20Art%20and%20Aesthetic.pdf, accessed January 21, 2020.

25 Kelly, M. (2016) *Kintsukuroi: Finding beauty in a broken world*. Available at www.youtube.com/watch?v=cL9qvklcNTY, accessed January 21, 2020.

26 Harris, A. (2015) *Kintsugi: The art of broken*. Available at www.youtube.com/watch?v=B-uZiszbo7M, accessed January 21, 2020.

Wellbeing Hack 8: Sleep for Eight Hours

1 Cartwright, R. D. (2010) *The Twenty-Four Hour Mind: The Role of Sleep and Dreaming in Our Emotional Lives*. Oxford: Oxford University Press.

2 Cartwright, R.D. (1991) 'Dreams that work: The relation of dream incorporation to adaptation to stressful events.' *Dreaming* 1(1), 3–9.

3 Nofzinger, E.A. (2005) 'Neuroimaging and sleep medicine.' *Sleep Medicine Reviews* 9(3), 157–172.

4 Goldstein, A.N. & Walker, M.P. (2014) 'The role of sleep in emotional brain function.' *Annual Review of Clinical Psychology* 10, 679–708.

5 van der Helm, E. & Walker, M.P. (2012) 'Sleep and affective brain regulation.' *Social and Personality Psychology Compass* 6(11), 773–791.

6 See note 4.

7 Payne, J.D., Chambers, A.M. & Kensinger, E.A. (2012) 'Sleep promotes lasting changes in selective memory for emotional scenes.' *Frontiers in Integrative Neuroscience* 6(108). DOI: 10.3389/fnint.2012.00108

8 Menza, M.M., Rihm, J.S., Salari, N., Born, J. *et al.* (2013) 'The role of sleep and sleep deprivation in consolidating fear memories.' *NeuroImage* 75, 87–96.

9 Walker, M. (2017) *Why We Sleep: The New Science of Sleep and Dreams.* London: Penguin.

10 van der Helm, E., Gujar, N. & Walker, M.P. (2010) 'Sleep deprivation impairs the accurate recognition of human emotions.' *Sleep* 33(3), 335–342.

11 Gujar, N., McDonald, S.A., Nishida, M. & Walker, M.P. (2011) 'A role for REM sleep in recalibrating the sensitivity of the human brain to specific emotions.' *Cerebral Cortex* 21(1), 115–123.

12 See note 4.

13 See note 9.

14 Ben Simon, E., Rossi, A., Harvey, A.G. & Walker, M.P. (2019) 'Overanxious and underslept.' *Nature Human Behaviour* 4, 100–110.

15 See note 4.

16 Chatterjee, R. & Walker, M. (2019) *Why sleep is the most important pillar of health.* Available at https://drchatterjee.com/why-sleep-is-the-most-important-pillar-of-health-with-professor-matthew-walker, accessed January 21, 2020.

17 Watson, N.F., Harden, K.P., Buchwald, D., Vitiello, M.V. *et al.* (2014) 'Sleep duration and depressive symptoms: A gene-environment interaction.' *Sleep* 37(2), 351–358.

18 Harvey, A. (2016) *Alison Harvey, Ph.D.* Available at www.youtube.com/watch?v=h YdqCka8cqc, accessed January 21, 2020.

19 Bernert, R.A., Kim, J.S., Iwata, N.G. & Perlis, M.L. (2015) 'Sleep disturbances as an evidence-based suicide risk factor.' *Current Psychiatry Reports* 17(3), 554.

20 See note 9.

21 See note 9.

22 Kemp-Habib, A. (2019) 'How to get a good night's sleep: The best and worst food and drink.' *The Times*, June 2, 2019. Available at www.thetimes.co.uk/article/good-bad-food-drink-sleep-well-caffeine-alcohol-disrupt-when-stop-eating-caffeine-ljqkt2x6j, accessed January 21, 2020.

23 See note 9.

24 Sundelin, T., Lekander, M. & Sorjonen, K. (2017) 'Negative effects of restricted sleep on facial appearance and social appeal.' *Royal Society Open Science* 4(5). DOI: 10.1098/rsos.160918

25 Beccutia, G. & Pannaina, S. (2011) 'Sleep and obesity.' *Current Opinion in Clinical Nutrition and Metabolic Care* 14(4), 402–412.

26 Liu, M.M., Liu, L., Chen, L., Yin, X.-J. *et al.* (2017) 'Sleep deprivation and late bedtime impair sperm health through increasing antisperm antibody production: A prospective study of 981 healthy men.' *Medical Science Monitor* 23, 1842–1848.

27 Kold Jensen, T., Andersson, A.M., Skakkebæk, N.E., Joensen, U.N. *et al.* (2013) 'Association of sleep disturbances with reduced semen quality: A cross-sectional study among 953 healthy young Danish men.' *American Journal of Epidemiology* 177(10), 1027–1037.

28 Cohen, S., Doyle, W.J., Alper, C.M, Janicki-Deverts, D. & Turner, R.B. (2009) 'Sleep habits and susceptibility to the common cold.' *Archives of Internal Medicine* 169(1), 62–67.

29 See note 9.

30 Shokri-Kojori, E., Wang, G.J., Wiers, C.E. *et al.* (2018) 'β-Amyloid accumulation in the human brain after one night of sleep deprivation.' *PNAS* 115(17), 4483–4488.

Wellbeing Hack 9: Stand on a Desk

1 Twenge, J.M. & Campbell, W.K. (2009) *The Narcissism Epidemic: Living in the Age of Entitlement.* New York, NY: Free Press.

2 Krizan, Z. & Herlache, A. (2017) 'The narcissism spectrum model: A synthetic view of narcissistic personality.' *Personality and Social Psychology Review 22*(1), 3–31.

3 Back, M., Schmukle, S. & Egloff, B. (2010) 'Why are narcissists so charming at first sight? Decoding the narcissism-popularity link at zero acquaintance.' *Journal of Personality and Social Psychology 98*(1), 132–145.

4 Besser, A. & Priel, B. (2010) 'Grandiose narcissism versus vulnerable narcissism in threatening situations: Emotional reactions to achievement failure and interpersonal rejection.' *Journal of Social and Clinical Psychology 29*(8), 874–902.

5 Miller, J.D., Hoffman, B.J., Gaughan, E.T., Gentile, B., Maples, J. & Keith Campbell, W. (2011) 'Grandiose and vulnerable narcissism: Anomological network analysis.' *Journal of Personality 79*(5), 1013–1042.

6 Wong, B. (n.d.) '8 undeniable signs you've fallen for a narcissist.' *Huffington Post.* Available at www.huffpost.com/entry/aint-nobody-got-time-for-a-narcissist-heres-how-to-avoid-dating-one_n_5696ea2ae4b0778f46f82652, accessed January 24, 2020.

7 See note 2.

8 Wink, P. (1991) 'Two faces of narcissism.' *Journal of Personality and Social Psychology 61*(4), 590–597.

9 Depression Alliance (n.d.) *Vulnerable narcissism: Understanding its role in today's society.* Available at www.depressionalliance.org/vulnerable-narcissism, accessed January 24, 2020.

10 See note 9.

11 See note 6.

12 See note 9.

13 Paulhus, D. & Williams, K. (2002) 'The Dark Triad of personality: Narcissism, Machiavellianism, and psychopathy.' *Journal of Research in Personality 36*(6), 556–563.

14 Furnham, A., Richards, S. & Paulhus, D. (2013) 'The Dark Triad of personality: A 10 year review.' *Social and Personality Psychology Compass 7*(3), 199–216.

15 Kaufman, S.B., Yaden, D.B. & Tsukayama, E. (2019) 'The light vs. dark triad of personality: Contrasting two very different profiles of human nature.' *Frontiers in Psychology 10*, 467.

16 See note 15.

17 See note 15.

18 See note 15.

19 See note 15.

20 Bermúdez, J.P. (2016) 'Practical reason, habit, and care in Aristotle.' *Praxis Filosófica Nueva 43*, 77–102.

21 Hudson, N., Roberts, B. & Lodi-Smith, J. (2012) 'Personality trait development and social investment in work.' *Journal of Research in Personality 46*(3), 334–344.

22 Hudson, N.W. & Fraley, C. (2015) 'Volitional personality trait change: Can people choose to change their personality traits?' *Journal of Personality and Social Psychology 109*(3), 490–507.

23 Hudson, N.W., Briley, D.A., Chopik, W.J. & Derringer, J. (2018) 'You have to follow through: Attaining behavioral change goals predicts volitional personality change.' *Journal of Personality and Social Psychology 117*(4), 839–857.

24 Jarrett, C. 'Merely desiring to alter your personality is not enough, and may backfire unless you take concrete action to change.' *British Psychological Society Research Digest.* Available at https://digest.bps.org.uk/2018/11/01/merely-desiring-to-alter-your-personality-is-not-enough-and-may-backfire-unless-you-take-concrete-action-to-change, accessed January 24, 2020.

25 See note 23.

26 See note 24.

27 Pine, K. (2016) 'The flextrovert advantage.' *Do Something Different*. Available at https://dsd.me/wp-content/uploads/2016/12/Do-Flextrovert-ebook-.pdf, accessed January 24, 2020.

28 Pine, K. (2017) *What it means to be a 'flextrovert'*. Available at www.youtube.com/watch?v=TWcW8f8oaaE, accessed January 24, 2020.

29 Cheng, C. & Cheung, M.W.L. (2005) 'Cognitive processes underlying coping flexibility: Differentiation and integration.' *Journal of Personality 73*(4), 859–886.

30 Klohnen, E. (1996) 'Conceptual analysis and measurement of the construct of ego-resiliency.' *Journal of Personality and Social Psychology 70*(5), 1067–1079.

31 Rottenberg, J. (2005) 'Mood and emotion in major depression.' *Current Directions in Psychological Science 14*(3), 167–170.

32 Borkovec, T.D. (1994) 'The Nature, Functions, and Origins of Worry.' In G. Davey and F. Tallis (eds) *Worrying: Perspectives on Theory, Assessment, and Treatment*. Chichester: Wiley and Sons.

33 Pine, K. & Fletcher, B. (2014) 'Time to shift brain channels to bring about effective changes in health behaviour.' *Perspectives in Public Health 134*(1), 16–17.

34 Feldner, M.T., Hekmat, H., Zvolensky, M.J., Vowles, K.E., Secrist, Z. & Leen-Feldner, E.W. (2006) 'The role of experiential avoidance in acute pain tolerance: A laboratory test.' *Journal of Behavior Therapy and Experimental Psychiatry 37*(2), 146–158.

35 Charlton, N., Pine, K. & Fletcher, B. (2016) *Diversity and inclusiveness, wellbeing and openness to change: The effects of a Do Something Different programme in a global organisation*. Available at https://dsd.me/business/wp-content/uploads/sites/12/2016/08/Diversity-and-inclusiveness-white-paper-1.pdf, accessed January 24, 2020.

36 Do Something Different (n.d.) *Live the life you want*. Available at https://dsd.me, accessed January 24, 2020.

37 Rotten Tomatoes (n.d.) *Dead Poets Society quotes*. Available at www.rottentomatoes.com/m/dead_poets_society/quotes, accessed January 24, 2020.

38 Spinner, J. (2003) 'Interview with Sam Pickering.' *Fourth Genre: Explorations in Nonfiction 5*(1), 192–207. Available at http://muse.jhu.edu/article/42687, accessed January 24, 2020.

Wellbeing Hack 10: Take A Forest Bath

1 Birkett, M.A. (2011) 'The Trier social stress test protocol for inducing psychological stress.' *Journal of Visualized Experiments 56*, 3238.

2 Thoma, M.V., La Marca, R., Brönnimann, L., Finkel, L., Ehlert, U. & Nater, M.L. (2013) 'The effect of music on the human stress response.' *PLoS One 8*(8). DOI: 10.1371/journal.pone.0070156

3 Lee, K.E., Williams, J.H., Sargent, L.D. Williams, N.S.G. & Johnson, K.A. (2015) '40-second green roof views sustain attention: The role of micro-breaks in attention restoration.' *Journal of Environmental Psychology 42*, 182–189.

4 Ulrich, R.S. (1984) 'View through a window may influence recovery from surgery.' *Science 224*(4647), 420–421.

5 Lee, M.S., Lee, J., Park B.J. & Miyazaki, Y. (2015) 'Interaction with indoor plants may reduce psychological and physiological stress by suppressing autonomic nervous system activity in young adults: A randomized crossover study.' *Journal of Physiological Anthropology 34*(21). DOI: 10.1186/s40101-015-0060-8

6 Largo-Wight, E.E., Chen, W.W., Dodd, V. & Weiler, R. (2011) 'Healthy workplaces: The effects of nature contact at work on employee stress and health.' *Public Health Reports 126*(Suppl. 1), 124–130.

7 O'Connor, A. (2010) 'The claim: Exposure to plants and parks can boost immunity.' *The New York Times*. Available at www.nytimes.com/2010/07/06/health/06real.html, accessed January 21, 2020.

8 Kuo, M. (2015) 'How might contact with nature promote human health? Promising mechanisms and a possible central pathway.' *Frontiers in Psychology 6*, 1093.

9 Morita, E., Fukuda, S., Nagano, J., Hamajima, N. *et al.* (2007) 'Psychological effects of forest environments on healthy adults: Shinrin-yoku (forest-air bathing, walking) as a possible method of stress reduction.' *Public Health 121*(1), 54–63.

10 Tsunetsugu, Y., Park, B.J., Ishii, H., Hirano, H., Kagawa, T. & Miyazaki, Y. (2007) 'Physiological effects of shinrin-yoku (taking in the atmosphere of the forest) in an old-growth broadleaf forest in Yamagata Prefecture, Japan.' *Journal of Physiological Anthropology 26*(2), 135–142.

11 Mao, G.X., Lan, X.G., Cao, Y.B., Chen, Z.M. *et al.* (2012) 'Effects of short-term forest bathing on human health in a broad-leaved evergreen forest in Zhejiang Province, China.' *Biomedical and Environmental Sciences 25*(3), 317–324.

12 Shanahan, D.F., Bush, R., Gaston, K.V., Lin, B.B. *et al.* (2016) 'Health benefits from nature experiences depend on dose.' *Scientific Reports 6*, 28551.

13 See note 8.

14 See note 8.

15 Repke, M.A., Berry, M.S., Conway, L.G., Metcalf, A., Hensen, R.M. & Phelan, C. (2018) 'How does nature exposure make people healthier?: Evidence for the role of impulsivity and expanded space perception.' *PloS One 13*(8), e0202246.

16 Wang, X.L., Li, C.R., Xu, J.W., Hu, D.M., Zhao, Z.L. & Zhang, L.D. (2013) 'Air negative ion concentration in different modes of courtyard forests in southern mountainous areas of Jinan, Shandong Province of East China.' *Journal of Applied Ecology 24*(2), 373–378.

17 Goel, N., Terman, M., Terman, J.S., Macchi, M.M. & Stewart, J.W. (2005) 'Controlled trial of bright light and negative air ions for chronic depression.' *Psychological Medicine 357*(7), 945–955.

18 See note 2.

19 Li, Q. (2018)'"Forest bathing" is great for your health. Here's how to do it.' *Time* magazine. Available at http://time.com/5259602/japanese-forest-bathing, accessed January 21, 2020.

Wellbeing Hack 11: Do (Almost) Nothing

1 Walker, M. (2017) *Why We Sleep: The New Science of Sleep and Dreams*. London: Penguin.

2 *Time* magazine (1979) *Business: The quintessential innovator*. Available at http://content.time.com/time/subscriber/article/0,33009,947523-1,00.html, accessed January 22, 2020.

3 Horowitz, A. (n.d.) *Dormio*. Available at www.adamjhh.com/dormio, accessed January 22, 2020.

4 Media.MIT (n.d.) *Dormio: Interfacing with dreams for creativity*. Available at www.media.mit.edu/projects/sleep-creativity/overview, accessed January 22, 2020.

5 National Trust (n.d.) *Isaac Newton's apple tree*. Available at www.nationaltrust.org.uk/woolsthorpe-manor/features/the-story-of-our-apple-tree-at-woolsthorpe-manor, accessed January 22, 2020.

6 Stukeley, W. (2004) *Revised memoir of Newton*. Available at www.NewtonProject.ox.ac.uk, accessed January 22, 2020.

7 Wilson, T., Reinhard, D.A., Westgate, E.C., Gilbert, D.T. *et al.* (2014) 'Just think: The challenges of the disengaged mind.' *Science 345*(6192), 75–77.

8 See note 7.

9 Alloy, A. & Abramson, L. (2007) 'The Adolescent Surge in Depression and Emergence of Gender Differences.' In D. Romer and E. Walker (eds) *Adolescent Psychopathology and the Developing Brain: Integrating Brain and Prevention Science*. Oxford: Oxford University Press.

10 Treynor, W., Gonzalez, R. & Nolen-Hoeksema, S. (2003) 'Rumination reconsidered: A psychometric analysis.' *Cognitive Therapy and Research 27*, 247–259.

11 See note 7.

12 Andrade, J. (2010) 'What does doodling do?' *Applied Cognitive Psychology 24*(1), 100–106.

13 Oppezzo, M. & Schwartz, D. (2014) 'Give your ideas some legs: The positive effect of walking.' *Journal of Experimental Psychology: Learning, Memory, and Cognition 40*(4), 1142–1152.

14 Kaimala, G., Ayaz, H., Herres, J., Dieterich-Hartwell, R. *et al.* (2017) 'Functional near-infrared spectroscopy assessment of reward perception based on visual self-expression: Coloring, doodling, and free drawing.' *The Arts in Psychotherapy 55*, 85–92.

15 Menon, V. (2015) 'Large-Scale Functional Brain Organization.' In A.W. Toga (ed.) *Brain Mapping: An Encyclopedic Reference, Vol. 2*. Cambridge, MA: Academic Press.

16 Beatya, R.E., Kennett, Y.N., Christensen, A.P., Rosenberg, M.D. *et al.* (2018) 'Robust prediction of individual creative ability from brain functional connectivity.' *PNAS 115*(5), 1087–1092.

17 Lewis, C.S. (1950) *The Lion, the Witch and the Wardrobe*. London: Puffin.

18 Erikson, E.H. (1968) *Identity: Youth and Crisis*. New York, NY: Norton.

19 Waters, T. & Fivush, R. (2015) 'Relations between narrative coherence, identity, and psychological well-being in emerging adulthood.' *Journal of Personality 83*(4), 441–451.

Wellbeing Hack 12: Take an Exercise Snack

1 Bergouignan, A., Legget, K.T., De Jong, N., Kealey, E. *et al.* (2016) 'Effect of frequent interruptions of prolonged sitting on self-perceived levels of energy, mood, food cravings and cognitive function.' *International Journal of Behavioral Nutrition and Physical Activity 13*(1), 113.

2 See note 1.

3 Oppezzo, M. & Schwartz, D. (2014) 'Give your ideas some legs: The positive effect of walking.' *Journal of Experimental Psychology: Learning, Memory, and Cognition 40*(4), 1142–1152.

4 Jenkins, E.M., Nairn, L.N., Skelly, L.E., Little, J.P. & Gibala, M.J. (2019) 'Do stair climbing exercise "snacks" improve cardiorespiratory fitness?' *Applied Physiology, Nutrition and Metabolism 44*(6), 681–684.

5 Wasmer Andrews, L. (2019) *Walk this way to tap into creative thinking*. Available at www.psychologytoday.com/us/blog/minding-the-body/201905/walk-way-tap-creative-thinking, accessed January 22, 2020.

6 Diaz, K.M., Howard, V.J., Hutto, B., Colabianchi, N. *et al.* (2017) 'Patterns of sedentary behavior and mortality in U.S. middle-aged and older adults: A national cohort study.' *Annals of Internal Medicine 167*(7), 465–475.

7 Zetlin, M. (2019) *Dancing benefits brain function teamwork and health, according to a neuroscience Ph.D.* Available at www.inc.com/minda-zetlin/dancing-dance-benefits-brain-function-teamwork-health-peter-lovatt-phd.html, accessed January 22, 2020.

8 Goldstein, B.I. & Young, L.T. (2013) 'Toward clinically applicable biomarkers in bipolar disorder: Focus on BDNF, inflammatory markers, and endothelial function.' *Current Psychiatry Reports 15*(12), 425.

9 Hosang, G.M., Shiles, C., Tansey, K.E., McGuffin, P. & Uher, R. (2014) 'Interaction between stress and the BDNF Val66Met polymorphism in depression: A systematic review and meta-analysis.' *BMC Medicine 12*, 7. DOI: 10.1186/1741-7015-12-7

10 Castrén, E., Võikar, V. & Rantamäki, T. (2007) 'Role of neurotrophic factors in depression.' *Current Opinion in Pharmocology 7*(1), 18–21.

11 Autry, A.E. & Monteggia, L.M. (2012) 'Brain-derived neurotrophic factor and neuropsychiatric disorders.' *Pharmacological Reviews 64*(2), 238–258.

12 Serra, G. & Fratta, W. (2007) 'A possible role for the endocannabinoid system in the neurobiology of depression.' *Clinical Practice and Epidemiology in Mental Health 3*, 25. DOI: 10.1186/1745-0179-3-25

13 Murawska-Cialowicz, E., Wojna, J. & Zuwala-Jagiello, J. (2015) 'Crossfit training changes brain-derived neurotrophic factor and irisin levels at rest, after wingate and progressive tests, and improves aerobic capacity and body composition of young physically active men and women.' *Journal of Physiology and Pharmocology 66*(6), 811–821.

14 Cabral-Santos, C., Castrillón, C.I., Miranda, R.A., Monteiro, P.A. *et al.* (2016) 'Inflammatory cytokines and BDNF response to high-intensity intermittent exercise: Effect the exercise volume.' *Frontiers in Physiology 7*, 509.

15 Ranjbar, E. Memari, A.M., Hafizi, S., Shayestehfar, M. *et al.* (2015) 'Depression and exercise: A clinical review and management guideline.' *Asian Journal of Sports Medicine 6*(2), e24055.

16 Aylett, E., Small, N. & Bower, P. (2018) 'Exercise in the treatment of clinical anxiety in general practice: A systematic review and meta-analysis.' *BMC Health Services Research 18*(1), 559.

17 Gordon, B.R., McDowell, C.P., Hallgren, M., Meyer, J.D., Lyons, M. & Herring, M.P. (2018) 'Association of efficacy of resistance exercise training with depressive symptoms: Meta-analysis and meta-regression analysis of randomized clinical trials.' *JAMA Psychiatry 75*(6), 566–576.

18 Ekberg, S. (2018) *Aerobic exercise vs anaerobic exercise.* Available at www.youtube.com/watch?v=lVeAK_muXsE, accessed January 22, 2020.

19 Slusher, A.L., Patterson, V.T., Schwartz, C.S. & Acevedo, E.O. (2018) 'Impact of high intensity interval exercise on executive function and brain derived neurotrophic factor in healthy college aged males.' *Physiology and Behavior 191*, 116–122.

20 DeLauer, T. (2018) *Most people do HIIT cardio wrong – how to do HIIT.* Available at www.youtube.com/watch?v=5O1TTduK6mw, accessed January 22, 2020.

21 Machado, A., Baker, J.S., Figueira Junior, A.J. & Bocalini, D.S. (2017) 'High-intensity interval training using whole-body exercises: Training recommendations and methodological overview.' *Clinical Physiology and Functional Imaging 39*(6), 378–383.

22 See note 20.

23 Gibala, M.J. & Jones, A.M. (2013) 'Physiological and performance adaptations to high-intensity interval training.' *Nestlé Nutrition Institute Workshop Series 76*, 51–60.

24 See note 21.

25 Ekberg, S. (2018) *Is HIIT better than steady cardio?* Available at www.youtube.com/watch?v=gnGalC6fXl4&list=PLpTTF6wMDLR4oA3p4U39Yli8D1ARPaFva&index=21&t=313s, accessed January 22, 2020.

26 See note 23.

27 Bhosle, S.G., Vardhan, V. & Mahajan, A. (2018) 'Effect of high intensity interval training with the use of trampoline in individuals with stress.' *International Journal of Physiotherapy and Research 6*(6), 2899–2904.

28 Ross, R. (2019) *Demystifying the endocannabinoid system.* Available at www.youtube.com/watch?v=8GsmTFytBYI, accessed January 22, 2020.

29 See note 28.

30 Kathuria, S., Gaetani, S., Fegley, D., Valiño, F. *et al.* (2003) 'Modulation of anxiety through blockade of anandamide hydrolysis.' *Nature Medicine 9*(1), 76–81.

31 Shonesy, B.C., Bluett, R.J., Ramikie, T.S., Báldi, R. *et al.* (2014) 'Genetic disruption of 2-arachidonoylglycerol synthesis reveals a key role for endocannabinoid signaling in anxiety modulation.' *Cell Reports 9*(5), 1644–1653.

32 Green, B., Kavanagh, D. & Young, R. (2003) 'Being stoned: A review of self-reported cannabis effects.' *Drug and Alcohol Review 22*(4), 453–460.

33 Volkow, N.D., Baler, R.D., Compton, W.M. & Weiss, S.R.B. (2016) 'Adverse health effects of marijuana use.' *The New England Journal of Medicine 370*(23), 2219–2227.

34 Morena, M., Patel, S., Bains, J.S. & Hill, M.N. (2016) 'Neurobiological interactions between stress and the endocannabinoid system.' *Neuropsychopharmacology 41*(1), 80–102.

35 See note 28.

36 See note 34.

37 Horder, J., Browning, M., Di Simplicio, M., Cowen, P.J. & Harmer, C.J. (2012) 'Effects of 7 days of treatment with the cannabinoid type 1 receptor antagonist, rimonabant, on emotional processing.' *Journal of Psychopharmacology 26*(1), 125–132.

38 Koltyn, K.F., Brellenthin, A.G., Cook, D.B., Sehgal, N. & Hillard, C. (2014) 'Mechanisms of exercise-induced hypoalgesia.' *The Journal of Pain 15*(12), 1294–1304.

39 Laskowski, E.R. (n.d.) *Are isometric exercises a good way to build strength?* Available at www.mayoclinic.org/healthy-lifestyle/fitness/expert-answers/isometric-exercises/faq-20058186, accessed January 22, 2020.

40 Raichlen, D.A., Foster, A.D., Seillier, A., Giuffrida, A. & Gerdeman, G.L. (2013) 'Exercise-induced endocannabinoid signaling is modulated by intensity.' *European Journal of Applied Physiology 113*(4), 869–875.

41 The Nutrition Source (n.d.) *Examples of moderate and vigorous physical activity.* Available at www.hsph.harvard.edu/obesity-prevention-source/moderate-and-vigorous-physical-activity, accessed January 22, 2020.

42 Raichlen, D.A., Foster, A.D., Gerdeman, G.L., Seillier, A. & Giuffrida, A. (2012) 'Wired to run: Exercise-induced endocannabinoid signaling in humans and cursorial mammals with implications for the "runner's high."' *Journal of Experimental Biology 215*, 1331–1336.

43 Heyman, E., Gamelin, F.X., Goekint, M., Piscitelli, F. *et al.* (2012) 'Intense exercise increases circulating endocannabinoid and BDNF levels in humans: Possible implications for reward and depression.' *Psychoneuroendocrinology 37*(6), 844–851.

44 D'Souza, D.C., Pittman, B., Perry, E. & Simen, A. (2009) 'Preliminary evidence of cannabinoid effects on brain-derived neurotrophic factor (BDNF) levels in humans.' *Psychopharmacology 202*(4), 569–578.

45 Choi, K.W., Chen, C.-Y., Stein, M.B., Klimentidis, Y.C. *et al.* (2018) 'Testing causal bidirectional influences between physical activity and depression using Mendelian randomization.' *JAMA Psychiatry*. DOI: 10.1001/jamapsychiatry.2018.4175

46 Miller, J.C. & Krizan, Z. (2016) 'Walking facilitates positive affect (even when expecting the opposite).' *Emotion 16*(5), 775–778.

Wellbeing Hack 13: Breathe Tactically

1 Kennedy, T. (2011) 'How combat breathing saved my life.' *Police*. Available at www.policemag.com/373760/how-combat-breathing-saved-my-life, accessed January 22, 2020.

2 Varga, S. & Heck, D.H. (2017) 'Rhythms of the body, rhythms of the brain: Respiration, neural oscillations, and embodied cognition.' *Consciousness and Cognition 56*, 77–90

3 Goyder, C. (2014) *The surprising secret to speaking with confidence*. Available at www.youtube.com/watch?v=a2MR5XbJtXU, accessed January 22, 2020.

4 Pollak, S.M. (2014) 'Email apnea: Breathing meditations for the workplace.' *Psychology Today*. Available at www.psychologytoday.com/gb/blog/the-art-now/201411/email-apnea, accessed January 22, 2020.

5 Zaccaro, A., Piarulli, A., Laurino, M., Garbella, E. *et al.* (2018) 'How breath-control can change your life: A systematic review on psycho-physiological correlates of slow breathing.' *Frontiers in Human Neuroscience 12*, 353.

6 Mohamed, L., Hanafy, N. & El-Naby, A. (2013) 'Effect of slow deep breathing exercise on blood pressure and heart rate among newly diagnosed patients with essential hypertension.' *Journal of Education and Practice 5*(4), 36–45.

7 Ma, X., Yue, Z.Q., Gong, Z.Q., Zhang, H. *et al.* (2017) 'The effect of diaphragmatic breathing on attention, negative affect and stress in healthy adults.' *Frontiers in Psychology 8*, 874. DOI: 10.3389/fpsyg.2017.00874

8 Zelano, C., Jiang, H., Zhou, G., Arora, N. *et al.* (2016) 'Nasal respiration entrains human limbic oscillations and modulates cognitive function.' *Journal of Neuroscience 36*(49), 12448–12467.

9 See note 8.

10 Huijbers, W., Pennartz, C.M., Beldzik, E., Domagalik, A. *et al.* (2014) 'Respiration phase-locks to fast stimulus presentations: Implications for the interpretation of posterior midline "deactivations".' *Human Brain Mapping 35*(9), 4932–4943.

11 Ebert, D., Hefter, H., Binkofski, F. & Freund, H.J. (2002) 'Coordination between breathing and mental grouping of pianistic finger movements.' *Perceptual and Motor Skills 95*(2), 339–353.

12 Arshamian, A., Iravani, B., Majid, A. & Lundström, J.N. (2018) 'Respiration modulates olfactory memory consolidation in humans.' *The Journal of Neuroscience 38*(48), 10286–10294.

13 Grossman, D. and Christensen, L.W. (2008) *On Combat: The Psychology and Physiology of Deadly Conflict in War and in Peace*. Breese, IL: Human Factor Research Group Inc.

14 Weil, A. (2014) *How to perform the 4-7-8 breathing exercise*. Available at www.youtube.com/watch?v=YRPh_GaiL8s&t=270s, accessed January 22, 2020.

15 Rockwood, L. (2018) *Change your breath, change your life*. Available at www.youtube.com/watch?v=_QTJOAIoUoU, accessed January 22, 2020.

16 *Iceman Wim Hof on Kilimanjaro summit* (2009). Available at www.youtube.com/watch?v=Bb2jJsi1Ykc, accessed January 22, 2020.

Wellbeing Hack 14: Stop Liking People

1 Wu, T. (2017) *The Attention Merchants: The Epic Struggle to Get Inside Our Heads*. New York, NY: Penguin Random House.

2 Banksy (2004) *Cut It Out*. UK: Weapons of Mass Destruction.

3 Skinner, B.F. (1965) *Science and Human Behavior*. New York, NY: Simon & Schuster.

4 Harris, T. (2019) *Tristan Harris – US Senate June 25, 2019*. Available at www.youtube.com/watch?v=WQMuxNiYoz4, accessed January 22, 2020.

5 Duhigg, C. (2012) *The Power of Habit: Why We Do What We Do and How to Change*. London: Random House.

6 Ikonn, M. (2019) *How to not get overwhelmed by social media*. Available at www.youtube.com/watch?v=YoLju7Z6o0U, accessed January 22, 2020.

7 Kahneman, D. (2011) *Thinking, Fast and Slow*. New York, NY: Penguin Random House.

8 See note 4.

9 Center for Humane Technology. *The Problem.* Available at www.HumaneTech.com/problem, accessed January 22, 2020.

10 Newport, C. (2019) *Digital Minimalism: Choosing a Focused Life in a Noisy World.* New York, NY: Portfolio/Penguin.

11 Shakya, H. & Christakis, N. (2017) 'Association of Facebook use with compromised well-being: A longitudinal study.' *American Journal of Epidemiology 185*(3), 203–211.

12 James, W. (1890) *Principles of Psychology.* New York, NY: Henry Holt and Company.

Wellbeing Hack 15: Join (or Leave) a Group

1 DEGOB (n.d) *The Holocaust in Hungary.* Available at http://degob.org/index.php?showarticle=2031, accessed January 22, 2020.

2 Arendt, H. (1963) *Eichmann in Jerusalem.* New York, NY: Viking Press.

3 Milgram, S. (1974) *Obedience to Authority: An Experimental View.* London: Tavistock Publications.

4 Cohen, R. (1999) 'Why? New Eichmann notes try to explain.' *The New York Times.* Available at www.nytimes.com/1999/08/13/world/why-new-eichmann-notes-try-to-explain.html, accessed January 22, 2020.

5 See note 3.

6 Reicher, S. (2018) *Professor Stephen Reicher on obedience.* Available at www.youtube.com/watch?v=RFOI6FJQBXY&t=1826s, accessed January 22, 2020.

7 See note 6.

8 Tajfel, H. and Turner, J.C. (1979) 'An Integrative Theory of Intergroup.' In W.G. Austin and S. Worchel (eds) *The Social Psychology of Intergroup Relations.* Monterey, CA: Brooks/Cole.

9 Haslam, A. (2018) 'Unlocking the social cure.' *The Psychologist 31*, 28–31.

10 Cesarani, D. (2006) *Becoming Eichmann: Rethinking the Life, Crimes, and Trial of a 'Desk Murderer'.* Boston, MA: Da Capo Press.

11 See note 3.

Wellbeing Hack 16: Ask Someone If They're Okay – Twice

1 Hampton, N. (2017) *All it takes is one.* Available at www.youtube.com/watch?v=sh7XFCysTr4, accessed January 22, 2020.

2 Henrich, J. & Henrich, N. (2006) 'Culture, evolution and the puzzle of human cooperation.' *Cognitive Systems Research 7*(2–3), 220–245.

3 Brown, W.M. & Consedine, N. (2005) 'Altruism relates to health in an ethnically diverse sample of older adults.' *The Journals of Gerontology: Series B, 60*(3), 143–152.

4 Schacter, H. & Margolin, G. (2018) 'When it feels good to give: Depressive symptoms, daily prosocial behavior, and adolescent mood.' *Emotion 19*(5), 923–927.

5 von Dawans, B., Fischbacher, U., Kirschbaum, C., Fehr, E. & Heinrichs, M. (2012) 'The social dimension of stress reactivity: Acute stress increases prosocial behavior in humans.' *Psychologial Science 23*(7), 829.

6 Alden, L.E. & Trew, J.L. (2013) 'If it makes you happy: Engaging in kind acts increases positive affect in socially anxious individuals.' *Emotion 13*(1), 64–75.

7 Layous, K., Nelson, S.K., Oberle, E., Schonert-Reichl, K.A. & Lyubomirsky, S. (2012) 'Kindness counts: Prompting prosocial behavior in preadolescents boosts peer acceptance and well-being.' *PLoS One 7*(12), e51380.

8 Gray, K. (2010) 'Moral transformation: Good and evil turn the weak into the mighty.' *Social Psychological and Personality Science 1*(3), 253–258.

9 Brown, B. & Brand, R. (2019) *Vulnerability & power.* Available at www.youtube.com/watch?v=SM1ckkGwqZI&t=1731s, accessed January 22, 2020.

10 Brown, B. (2013) *Brené Brown: 3 ways to set boundaries.* Available at www.oprah.com/spirit/how-to-set-boundaries-brene-browns-advice, accessed January 22, 2020.

11 Layous, K., Lee, H.J., Choi, I. & Lyubomirsky, S. (2013) 'Culture matters when designing a successful happiness-increasing activity: A comparison of the United States and South Korea.' *Journal of Cross-Cultural Psychology 44*(8), 1294–1303.

12 See note 6.

13 Lyubomirsky, S. & Layous, K.(2013) 'How do simple positive activities increase well-being?' *Current Directions in Psychological Science 22*(1), 57–62.

14 Aknin, L.B., Dunn, E.W., Whillans, A.V., Grant, A.M. & Norton, M.I. (2013) 'Making a difference matters: Impact unlocks the emotional benefits of prosocial spending.' *Journal of Economic Behavior and Organization 88*, 90–95.

15 Time to Change (n.d.) *Ask twice.* Available at www.time-to-change.org.uk/asktwice, accessed January 22, 2020.

16 *Cinderella* (2015) Disney film. 'Have courage and be kind.' Available at www.movie quotesandmore.com/cinderella-quotes, accessed December 4, 2019.

17 Weir, K. (2012) *The pain of social rejection.* American Psychological Association. Available at www.apa.org/monitor/2012/04/rejection, accessed January 22, 2020.

18 Gonsalkorale, K. & Williams, K.D. (2007) 'The KKK won't let me play: Ostracism even by a despised outgroup hurts.' *European Journal of Social Psychology 37*(6), 1176–1186.

19 Arbor, A. (2011) *Study illuminates the 'pain' of social rejection.* University of Michigan. Available at https://news.umich.edu/study-illuminates-the-pain-of-social-rejection, accessed January 22, 2020.

20 See note 9.

21 Winch, G. (2015) *Why rejection hurts so much – and what to do about it.* Available at https://ideas.ted.com/why-rejection-hurts-so-much-and-what-to-do-about-it, accessed January 22, 2020.

22 Vincenty, S. (2019) 'How to deal with rejection.' *O, the Oprah Magazine.* Available at www.oprahmag.com/life/a28225023/how-to-deal-with-rejection, accessed January 22, 2020.

23 Roosevelt, R. (1910) *Man in the arena speech: 'Citizenship in a Republic', delivered at the Sorbonne, in Paris, France on 23 April, 1910.* Available at www.worldfuturefund.org/Documents/maninarena.htm, accessed January 22, 2020.

24 See note 23.

Wellbeing Hack 17: Thank Your Way Out of Chaos

1   Keneally, M. (2019) *A look back at Trump comments perceived by some as encouraging violence.* Available at https://abcnews.go.com/Politics/back-trump-comments-perceived encouraging-violence/story?id=48415766, accessed January 23, 2020.

2   Reilly, K. (2016) 'Read Hillary Clinton's "basket of deplorables" remarks about Donald Trump supporters.' *Time* magazine. Available at https://time.com/4486502/hillary-clinton-basket-of-deplorables-transcript, accessed January 23, 2020.

3   Penny, L. (2016) 'I want my country back.' *The New Statesman.* Available at www.newstatesman.com/politics/uk/2016/06/i-want-my-country-back, accessed January 23, 2020.

4   Elgo, J. (2019) 'David Lammy says comparing ERG to Nazis "not strong enough".' *The Guardian.* Available at www.theguardian.com/politics/2019/apr/14/comparing-erg-to-nazis-not-strong-enough-says-david-lammy, accessed January 23, 2020.

5   Lineker (2016) *Twitter.* Available at https://twitter.com/garylineker/status/746293306670350336?lang=en, accessed January 23, 2020.

6   Corden, J. (2019) *Twitter.* Available at https://twitter.com/JKCorden/status/746192723506434048, accessed January 23, 2020.

7 *Good Morning Britain* (2019) *Should you lose your right to vote age 70?* Available at www.youtube.com/watch?v=WFLpDQSOgdk, accessed January 23, 2020.

8 Equality and Human Right Commission (2019) *Free speech to be protected at university*. Available at www.equalityhumanrights.com/en/our-work/news/free-speech-be-protected-university, accessed January 23, 2020.

9 Morris, S. (2015) 'Germaine Greer gives university lecture despite campaign to silence her.' *The Guardian*. Available at www.theguardian.com/books/2015/nov/18/transgender-activists-protest-germaine-greer-lecture-cardiff-university, accessed January 23, 2020.

10 Greer, G. (2015) *Germaine Greer: Transgender women are 'not women'*. BBC *Newsnight*. Available at www.youtube.com/watch?v=7B8Q6D4a6TM, accessed January 23, 2020.

11 Noor, M., Vollhardt, J., Mari, S. & Nadler, A. (2017) 'The social psychology of collective victimhood.' *European Journal of Social Psychology 47*(2), 121–134.

12 See note 11.

13 Bar-Tal, D., Chernyak-Hai, L., Schori, N. & Gundar, A. (2009) 'A sense of self-perceived collective victimhood in intractable conflicts.' *International Review of the Red Cross 91*(874), 229–258.

14 Richins, M.L. & Dawson, S. (1992) 'A consumer values orientation for materialism and its measurement: Scale development and validation.' *Journal of Consumer Research 19*(3), 303–316.

15 Kasser, T. (2002) *The High Price of Materialism*. Cambridge, MA: MIT Press.

16 Kasser, T. & Ryan, R.M. (1993) 'A dark side of the American dream: Correlates of financial success as a central life aspiration.' *Journal of Personality and Social Psychology 65*(2), 410–422.

17 Kasser, T. (2005) 'Frugality, Generosity, and Materialism in Children and Adolescents.' In K.A. Moore & L.H. Lippman (eds) *What Do Children Need to Flourish?: Conceptualizing and Measuring Indicators of Positive Development*. New York, NY: Kluwer/Plenum.

18 Poelker, K.E., Gibbons, J.L., Hughes, H.M. & Powlishta, K.K. (2006) 'Feeling grateful and envious: Adolescents' narratives of social emotions in identity and social development.' *International Journal of Adolescence and Youth 23*(3), 289–303.

19 McCullough, M.E., Emmons, R.A. & Tsang, J.-A. (2002) 'The grateful disposition: A conceptual and empirical topography.' *Journal of Personality and Social Psychology 82*, 112–127.

20 Kneezel, T. & Emmons, R.A. (2006) 'Personality and Spiritual Development.' In E.C. Roehlkepartain, P. Ebstyne King, L.M. Wagener & P.L. Benson (eds) *The Handbook of Spiritual Development in Childhood and Adolescence*. Thousand Oaks, CA: Sage Publications.

21 McCullough, M.E., Kimeldorf, M.B. & Cohen, A.D. (2008) 'An adaptation for altruism? The social causes, social effects, and social evolution of gratitude.' *Current Directions in Psychological Science 17*(4), 281–285.

22 Emmons, R.A. & Mishra, A. (2011) 'Why Gratitude Enhances Well-being: What We Know, What We Need to Know.' In T.B. Kashdan, M.F. Steger & K.M. Sheldon (eds) *Designing Positive Psychology: Taking Stock and Moving Forward*. Oxford: Oxford Scholarship Online.

23 Emmons, R.A. & McCullough, M.E. (2003) 'Counting blessings versus burdens: An experimental investigation of gratitude and subjective well-being in daily life.' *Journal of Personality and Social Psychology 84*(2), 377–389.

24 Emmons, R. (2013) *How gratitude can help you through hard times*. Available at https://greatergood.berkeley.edu/article/item/how_gratitude_can_help_you_through_hard_times, accessed January 23, 2020.

25 Harris, S. (2018) *Inspirational speech on gratitude.* Available at www.youtube.com/watch?v=Nb2FIP0kWpM, accessed January 23, 2020.

26 Frias, A., Watkins, P.C., Webber, A.C. & Froh, J.J. (2011) 'Death and gratitude: Death reflection enhances gratitude.' *The Journal of Positive Psychology* 6(2), 154–162.

27 Kennelly, S. (2014) *When guilt stops gratitude.* Available at https://greatergood.berkeley.edu/article/item/when_guilt_stops_gratitude, accessed January 23, 2020.

28 Koo, M., Algoe, S.B., Wilson, T.D. & Gilbert, D.T. (2008) 'It's a wonderful life: Mentally subtracting positive events improves people's affective states, contrary to their affective forecasts.' *Journal of Personality and Social Psychology* 95(5), 1217–1224.

29 Lambert, N.M., Graham, S.M. & Fincham, F.D. (2009) 'A prototype analysis of gratitude: Varieties of gratitude experiences.' *Personality and Social Psychology Bulletin* 35(9), 1193–1207.

30 Keltner, D. & Haidt, J. (2003) 'Approaching awe, a moral, spiritual, and aesthetic emotion.' *Cognition and Emotion* 17(2), 297–314.

31 Allen, S. (2018) *The science of awe.* Greater Good Science Center at UC Berkeley. Available at https://ggsc.berkeley.edu/images/uploads/GGSC-JTF_White_Paper-Awe_FINAL.pdf, accessed January 23 2020.

32 Algoe, S.B., Haidt, J. & Gable, S.L. (2008) 'Beyond reciprocity: Gratitude and relationships in every-day life.' *Emotion* 8(3), 425–429.

Wellbeing Hack 18: Hug Someone Real

1   Green, C.D. (n.d.) '"Conditioned emotional reactions" by John B. Watson and Rosalie Rayner (1920). First published in *Journal of Experimental Psychology* 3(1), 1–14.' *Classics in the History of Psychology,* available at https://psychclassics.yorku.ca/Watson/emotion.htm, accessed April 13, 2020.

2   Watson, J.B. (1928) *Psychological Care of Infant and Child.* New York, NY: Norton & Co.

3   Hannush, M. (1987) 'John B. Watson remembered: An interview with James B. Watson.' *Journal of the History of Behavioural Sciences* 23(2), 137–152.

4   Association for Psychological Science (2018) *Harlow's classic studies revealed the importance of maternal contact.* Available at www.psychologicalscience.org/publications/observer/obsonline/harlows-classic-studies-revealed-the-importance-of-maternal-contact.html, accessed January 23, 2020.

5   Linden, D. (2016) *The science of touching and feeling.* Available at www.youtube.com/watch?v=lW8pJ7E9taQ, accessed January 23, 2020.

6   Weir, K. (2014) 'The lasting impact of neglect.' *Monitor on Psychology* 45(6), 36.

7   See note 5.

8   Burgoon, J.K., Buller, D.B. & Woodall, W.G. (1996) *Nonverbal Communication: The Unspoken Dialogue.* New York, NY: McGraw-Hill.

9   See note 5.

10 Pawling, R., Cannon, P.R., McGlone, F.P. & Walker, S.C. (2017) 'C-tactile afferent stimulating touch carries a positive affective value.' *PLoS One* 12(3), e0173457.

11 Coan, J.A., Schaefer, H.S. & Davidson, R.J. (2006) 'Lending a hand: Social regulation of the neural response to threat.' *Psychological Science* 7(12), 1032–1039.

12 See note 11.

13 Light, K.C., Grewen, K.M. & Amico, J.A. (2005) 'More frequent partner hugs and higher oxytocin levels are linked to lower blood pressure and heart rate in premenopausal women.' *Biological Psychology* 69(1), 5–21.

14 Cohen, S., Janicki-Deverts, D., Turner, R.B. & Doyle, W.J. (2015) 'Does hugging provide stress-buffering social support? A study of susceptibility to upper respiratory infection and illness.' *Psychological Science* 26(2), 135–147.

15 Murphy, M.L.M., Janicki-Deverts, D. & Cohen, S. (2018) 'Receiving a hug is associated with the attenuation of negative mood that occurs on days with interpersonal conflict.' *PLoS One 13*(10), e0203522.

16 Holt-Lunstad, J., Birmingham, W.A. & Light, K.C. (2008) 'Influence of a "warm touch" support enhancement intervention among married couples on ambulatory blood pressure, oxytocin, alpha amylase, and cortisol.' *Psychosomatic Medicine 70*(9), 976–985.

17 Resnick, B. (2019) *Oxytocin, the so-called 'hug hormone,' is way more sophisticated than we thought.* Available at www.vox.com/science-and-health/2019/2/13/18221876/oxytocin-morality-valentines, accessed January 23, 2020.

18 De Waal, F. (1989) *Peacemaking among Primates.* Cambridge, MA: Harvard University Press.

19 Kraus, M.W., Huang, C. & Keltner, D. (2010) 'Tactile communication, cooperation, and performance: An ethological study of the NBA.' *Emotion 10*(5), 745–749.

20 Williams, L.E. & Bargh, J.A. (2008) 'Experiencing physical warmth promotes interpersonal warmth.' *Science 322*(5901), 606–607.

21 Guéguen, N. (2007) 'Courtship compliance: The effect of touch on women's behavior.' *Social Influence 2*(2), 81–97.

22 See note 21.

23 Crusco, A.H. & Wetzel, C.G. (1984) 'The Midas touch: The effects of interpersonal touch on restaurant tipping.' *Personality and Social Psychology Bulletin 10*, 512–517.

24 Cocksedge, S., George, B., Renwick, S. & Chew-Graham, C.A. (2013) 'Touch in primary care consultations: Qualitative investigation of doctors' and patients' perceptions.' *British Journal of General Practice 63*(609), e283-90.

25 Suvilehto, J., Glerean, E., Dunbar, R.I., Hari, R. & Nummenmaa, L. (2015) 'Topography of social touching depends on emotional bonds between humans.' *Psychological and Cognitive Sciences 112*(45), 13811–13816.

26 Lee, J.W. & Guerrero, L.K. (2001) 'Types of touch in cross-sex relationships between coworkers: Perceptions of relational and emotional messages, inappropriateness, and sexual harassment.' *Journal of Applied Communication Research 29*(3), 197–220.

27 Sakson-Obada, O. (2014) 'Body ego and trauma as correlates of comfort in the physical proximity of others.' *Polish Psychological Bulletin 45*(1), 92–100.

28 Wilhelm, F.H., Kochar, A.S., Roth, W.T. & Gross, J.J. (2001) 'Social anxiety and response to touch: Incongruence between self-evaluative and physiological reactions.' *Biological Psychology 58*(3), 181–202.

29 Butler, M.H., Pereyra, S.A., Draper, T.W., Leonhardt, N.D. & Skinner, K.B. (2018) 'Pornography use and loneliness: A bidirectional recursive model and pilot investigation.' *Journal of Sex and Marital Therapy 44*(2), 127–137.

30 Willoughby, B.J., Young-Petersen, B. & Leonhardt, N.D. (2017) 'Exploring trajectories of pornography use through adolescence and emerging adulthood.' *The Journal of Sex Research 55*(3), 1–13.